OBJECTIVES FOR
INSTRUCTION AND EVALUATION

OBJECTIVES
for INSTRUCTION
and EVALUATION

ROBERT J. KIBLER
Florida State University

DONALD J. CEGALA
Ohio State University

DAVID T. MILES
Southern Illinois University

LARRY L. BARKER
Florida State University

ALLYN and BACON Inc.
Boston • London • Sydney

CONTENTS

PREFACE

This book is intended as a supplementary text for most courses in education (for example, educational methods, educational psychology, psychology of learning, educational administration, philosophy of education, programed instruction, computer-based instruction, and methods of evaluation). Teachers, administrators, curriculum planners, members of school boards, and researchers also should find it of value.

Educational objectives have been studied throughout the history of American education. The work in programed learning and instructional technology in recent years has heightened interest in the specification of precise objectives. Efforts by Tyler (1934), Bloom et al. (1956), Mager (1962 and 1968), Mager and Beach (1967), Krathwohl et al. (1964), Gagné (1965a, 1965b, and 1970), Glaser (1962 and 1965), Popham (1969), and Popham and Baker (1970) have been most influential in this trend.

This book represents an effort to identify the important functions that instructional objectives can serve in improving instruction. We hope the book will contribute to the continuing effort to improve the quality and efficiency of instruction by shaping favorable attitudes toward the use of instructional objectives, by informing individuals about the nature and characteristics of objectives, and by helping educators write objectives.

This book makes six unique contributions:

1. It provides in a single volume material relative to instructional objectives gleaned from a variety of sources.
2. It presents a classroom-tested model of instruction that illustrates the relationships of instructional objectives to the instruction-learning process.

3. It prescribes an approach to objectives based on planning instruction and informing others of instructional goals.
4. It analyzes, in substantially more detail than has been available to date, the elements contained in objectives that are required to plan instruction.
5. It describes procedures for matching objectives and evaluation strategies.
6. It examines the relationship between instructional objectives, criterion-referenced evaluation, and mastery learning.

The authors express their appreciation to several persons who contributed to this text: first, to all the individuals who graciously permitted us to reprint their materials; second, to all the publishers and institutions who granted us permission to reproduce copyrighted materials, particularly the David McKay Company, the Instructional Objectives Exchange, and the CTB/McGraw-Hill Company; third, to Ronald E. Bassett for his uncommonly valuable assistance in preparing parts of the manuscript; and fourth, to Esther M. Cegala for typing the manuscript and for her patience and understanding during its preparation.

1

INSTRUCTIONAL OBJECTIVES AND THE INSTRUCTIONAL PROCESS

After completing this chapter, the learner should be able to:

1. Define the term instructional objectives;
2. Describe ten reasons for using instructional objectives in education;
3. Describe the current status of empirical research on instructional objectives;
4. Identify three methodological weaknesses characterizing empirical research on instructional objectives which may account for inconsistent research findings;
5. Identify fourteen key points of controversy over the use of instructional objectives;
6. State the major premise and specific assumptions underlying the general model of instruction;
7. Draw the general model of instruction and briefly describe each component in the model.

This chapter is divided into two major parts. In the first part we present a general rationale for using instructional objectives. We examine the reasons for using instructional objectives from three perspectives: a rational (or intuitive) perspective, an empirical perspective, and a functional perspective. In the second part of the chapter an overview of the general model of instruction is presented. Each component of the instructional model is described briefly and is related to instructional objectives.

1

THE RATIONALE FOR INSTRUCTIONAL OBJECTIVES
AND THEIR USE

Since the major focus of this book is on the nature and use of instructional objectives, it will be helpful to clarify at the outset what we mean by the term *instructional objective.* Instructional objectives are statements that describe what students will be able to do after completing a prescribed unit of instruction. Other terms that have been used to describe these types of objectives (i.e., instructional) are *behavioral objectives* and *performance goals.* The terms *behavioral* and *performance* often are used to describe objectives of the nature we will examine because the objectives inform students what behaviors, or performances (e.g., write an essay, draw a diagram, construct a model), they are expected to achieve to demonstrate that they have learned what is required of them.

Since chapter 2 is devoted to a detailed examination of instructional objectives, we will not take time here to describe the characteristics and components of instructional objectives. However, an example of an instructional objective at this point would probably be useful to establish a common meaning for the term. Below are two objectives; the first is *not* an instructional objective, while the second one is (additional sample objectives are provided in Appendix A):

1. The student will know what factors gave rise to the Industrial Revolution.
2. The student will list and describe in writing at least three factors that gave rise to the Industrial Revolution.

It should be clear that the second objective informs the student what he/she is to *do* (i.e., list and describe in writing at least three factors that gave rise to the Industrial Revolution) to demonstrate that learning has occurred. The first objective lacks specificity; it does not indicate *how* the student is to demonstrate what he/she knows and to what extent he/she is to know the required information. Additional distinguishing characteristics of instructional objectives will be presented and discussed later. If we are in general agreement as to what is meant by the term *instructional objective,* let us move on to a consideration of the various reasons for using instructional objectives.

Rational Basis for Using Instructional Objectives

In discussing the relative merits and problems of instructional objectives, many educators have pointed out several cogent reasons for using instructional objectives at all levels of education (e.g., elementary, secondary, and higher education). Among the more compelling reasons is that the use of instructional objectives is consistent with the concept of accountability (the balancing of money spent for education to amount of student learning). Accountability in education is rapidly gaining acceptance from both the public and the federal government. The publicity given the Texarkana program (Elam, 1970) and others like it has stimulated the belief that application of accountability concepts to public education is a "concrete practical activity" that may be used to confront some of the most critical educational dilemmas, including the re-establishment of confidence in the educational system at all levels (Lessinger, 1970). Even so, some educators perceive accountability as a threat to the educational process. Unfortunately, some educators who have negative attitudes about accountability also have become negative about instructional objectives. Apparently, the negative attitudes about instructional objectives are based on the misconception that using instructional objectives leads to accountability in education. Certainly the use of instructional objectives is consistent with accountability, but national and local economic considerations, rather than the use of instructional objectives itself, probably lead to, if they do not directly cause, accountability-based educational systems. Moreover, it is clear that some form of accountability may be inevitable given the current status of economic conditions and growing involvement of parent groups in making decisions about local educational systems.

Few comforting words can be said to those teachers who view accountability-based educational systems as a threat. However, if accountability-based educational systems do become the norm, experience in the use of instructional objectives will enable teachers to adapt to the system more easily. To achieve the balance between spending and student learning that accountability demands, the individual teacher or school system must be able to demonstrate that students have learned as a result of their instruction. Accordingly, educational accountability can be implemented successfully only if educational goals or objectives are precisely identified and stated before the instructional program begins and if some reliable measure of effectiveness of instruction in implementing these goals is devised. Development and use of instructional objectives will allow teachers to state their specific instructional goals to their immediate supervisors and school boards and will aid the teacher in developing effective means for assessing student attainment of the specified goals (as we shall see in chapter 6).

While the issue of accountability is one of the strongest reasons for using instructional objectives, there are additional reasons for their use in the educational process (Kibler and Barker, 1970; Kibler, Barker, and Cegala, 1970b). Among the additional reasons for using instructional objectives are the following:

1. Because instructional objectives clearly specify to students what is to be learned and how they are to demonstrate learning (including a statement of the criteria to be used in evaluating learners' performance), it seems reasonable to argue that students are spared the frustration and time-consuming effort of trying to guess what the teacher expects of them. Moreover, it appears logical that students will learn more easily if they are told what they are expected to learn and how they will be expected to demonstrate that learning has occurred.
2. Given such clearly specified objectives, curriculum planners are better able to arrange sequences of courses or units of instruction. Knowing what students (hopefully all students) will be able to do at the end of courses and what students are able to do at the beginning of courses (prerequisites) should make it possible to eliminate unnecessary overlap of courses and to identify and fill in gaps between courses.
3. Students and their advisors are able to plan their course programs better when they can read course descriptions that include instructional objectives.
4. Through clear instructional objectives, teachers are able to tell other teachers what they teach. Stating that "students learn to name each state and its capital in the United States" communicates considerably more than stating "United States geography is taught."
5. Teachers and administrators can determine the level of objectives students will be able to achieve in terms of the three taxonomic classifications to be discussed in chapter 5. For example, in the cognitive domain, objectives can be classified as knowledge, comprehension, application, analysis, synthesis, and evaluation, thereby avoiding undue emphasis on a certain level of objectives.
6. Given clearly defined goals to work toward, teachers can design instructional experiences to achieve them and can evaluate the effectiveness of such experiences according to whether the goals are achieved.

7. Gagné (1965a) has pointed out the necessity of evaluating student accomplishments in any educational program. It is important for the teacher to be able to determine the student's capabilities at any given time during an instructional program. When instructional objectives are specified, it is possible for the teacher to determine the student's present level of mastery for any prescribed objective at any time. Moreover, by specifying instructional objectives, teachers can identify a student who has acquired, prior to instruction, the level of excellence required for successful performance on a given objective. Instructional objectives also may help in identifying students who lack the prerequisites to master the prescribed objectives successfully.

8. Because an instructional objective includes a performance standard, it represents a minimal level of performance to be sought by all, or most, students. Therefore, most students in a given class can be expected to master successfully the behavior specified in an objective. This idea may seem startling—that most students in a class can succeed. However, such outstanding psychologists as Bloom (1968) and Carroll (1963) have argued that most students can achieve mastery if they will (and are permitted to) devote enough time to the learning task and if appropriate instruction is provided.

9. Performance standards also help teachers determine the adequacy of their instructional program. If students do not master objectives efficiently as a result of a given instructional program, various changes may be required in the program, in the objectives, or in other elements of the instructional process.

Empirical Basis for Using Instructional Objectives

Although there are several reasons on logical grounds for using instructional objectives, there is limited empirical data to support their unqualified use. Educators have given considerable attention to discussions about instructional objectives in the literature (see Poulliotte and Peters, 1971, and Geis, 1972, for extensive bibliographies), but there have been only fifty or so experimental studies focused on instructional objectives. Unfortunately, the results of these studies are inconsistent and provide no conclusive evidence about the effect of instructional objectives on learning.

A review of over fifty empirical studies of the effects of instructional objectives on student achievement suggests that current findings may be grouped into four separate categories.[1] The first category consists of investigations into the effects of student possession of instructional objectives on learning. The results of these studies overall provide no conclusive findings. Of the thirty-three studies found that compared student learning with and without possession of instructional objectives, only eleven reported that knowledge of instructional objectives improved learning significantly (Doty, 1968; Engel, 1968; Blaney and McKie, 1969; Dalis, 1970; Kueter, 1970; Lawrence, 1970; Nelson, 1970; Puckett, 1971; Webb, 1971; Ferre, 1972; and Olsen, 1972). Twenty-two other studies found no differential effects on learning that could be attributed to student possession of instructional objectives (Smith, 1967; Baker, 1969; Bishop, 1969; Boardman, 1970; Brown, 1970; Bryant, 1970; Conlon, 1970; Stedman, 1970; Weinberg, 1970; Hershman, 1971; Jenkins and Deno, 1971; Jordan, 1971; Lovett, 1971; Merrill and Towle, 1971; Olson, 1971; Phillips, 1971; Rowan, 1971; Clingman, 1972; Kalish, 1972; Loh, 1972; Patton, 1972; and Zimmerman, 1972).

The second category of studies consists of investigations into the effects of the form of instructional objectives (i.e., specific vs. general objectives) on student learning. The collective results of these studies suggest that there are no differential effects on student learning attributable to the form in which objectives are stated. Only two studies (Dalis, 1970, and Janeczko, 1971) found that students who receive specific instructional objectives (i.e., statements of terminal behaviors to be performed and conditions for performance) achieved significantly higher scores on a test of learning than students receiving more general objectives. Other studies found no differential effects related to objective form (Oswald and Fletcher, 1970; Stedman, 1970; Weinberg, 1970; Jenkins and Deno, 1971; and Lovett, 1971).

A third category includes investigations into the effects on student learning of teacher possession and use of instructional objectives. Of the eight studies included in this category, five found no significant effects on student achievement (Baker, 1969; Cardarelli, 1971; Crooks, 1971; Clingman, 1972; and Kalish, 1972), while three studies reported significant positive effects (Wittrock, 1962; McNeil, 1967; and Piatt, 1969).

Investigations in the fourth category focused on the effects of student possession of instructional objectives on efficiency (in terms of time) of

---

[1]The authors are indebted to Ronald E. Bassett for the following review of the literature on instructional objectives.

student learning. These studies also provide no conclusive findings. Two studies (Mager and McCann, 1961; Allen and McDonald, 1963) found that the use of instructional objectives significantly reduced the amount of time spent on learning, while five studies found no difference in learning time between students who had objectives and those who did not (Smith, 1970; Janeczko, 1971; Merrill and Towle, 1971; Rowan, 1971; and Loh, 1972).

Although less than half of the studies reported in the literature found support for the use of instructional objectives, a close examination of the research on the whole reveals a number of methodological weaknesses that may explain some of the inconsistent findings. Three methodological concerns seem particularly worthy of comment here. First, the ways of operationalizing instructional objectives are not standard across the experimental studies. Since researchers often do not report examples of instructional objectives used in the studies, it is difficult, if not impossible, to determine the worth of the objectives used. Second, very few researchers have provided subjects with instruction in the use of objectives prior to experimental treatment conditions. Since instructional objectives are new to most students, prior training in the use of objectives may be an important factor in determining how objectives affect student learning (Tiemann, 1968; Boardman, 1970; Brown, 1970; Jenkins and Deno, 1971; and Tobias and Duchastel, 1972). Only recently, Bassett's (1973) research has indicated that prior training in the use of instructional objectives influences learner performance within a modified mastery-learning system. Our experiences in using instructional objectives in our classes also support this notion. Appendix B contains a programed text designed to teach students how to use instructional objectives. The reader may find this

---

BRANCHING OPTION ONE

At this point in the text, the reader has the option of turning to additional material contained in Appendix B. You may find reading the material most beneficial at this point for purposes of clarity or you may choose to complete the reading of this section and branch to the material in the Appendix at a later time.

program or some variation of it useful in teaching students how to benefit maximally from instructional objectives. Third, few researchers have provided teachers with training in using instructional objectives. Consequently, it is difficult to determine if objectives were used appropriately in several of the reported studies.

In summary, current findings on the effects of instructional objectives provide no conclusive data on the relationship between the use of objectives and student learning. While instructional objectives have been found to facilitate learning in a number of studies, the facilitating effect has not been consistent across all studies. Consequently, we cannot, at this time, draw any conclusive generalization about the effect of instructional objectives on learning. However, despite this state of affairs there are several compelling reasons, on logical grounds, for using instructional objectives. We already have presented the most cogent of these reasons in the preceding section. Even so, there are a number of educators who perceive equally logical reasons for not using instructional objectives (Hausdorf, 1965; Eisner, 1967; Ebel, 1970; Macdonald and Walfron, 1970). The controversy over instructional objectives has generated several heated discussions among educators regarding whether or not objectives are either important or useful. Since the controversy over instructional objectives cannot be resolved at this time by an examination of the empirical data on the subject, we must turn to other ways of resolving the conflict.

Functional Basis for Using Instructional Objectives

Many of the controversies about instructional objectives stem either from differing philosophical views about the nature of education or from questions about how instructional objectives are applied to certain areas of education, such as the fine arts and humanities. In essence, the controversy often focuses on differing viewpoints about how instructional objectives function in an educational system. W. James Popham has written an insightful paper dealing with several arguments that have been presented in opposition to instructional objectives. Dr. Popham's paper is reproduced below as an introduction to some of the key points of controversy over the use of instructional objectives.

PROBING THE VALIDITY OF ARGUMENTS AGAINST
BEHAVIORAL GOALS*

W. James Popham
University of California, Los Angeles
Southwest Regional Laboratory
for Educational Research and Development

Within the last few years a rather intense debate has developed in the field of curriculum and instruction regarding the merits of stating instructional objectives in terms of measurable learner behaviors. Because I am thoroughly committed, both rationally and viscerally, to the proposition that instructional goals should be stated behaviorally, I view this debate with some ambivalence. On the one hand, it is probably desirable to have a dialogue of this sort among specialists in our field. We get to know each other better—between attacks. We test the respective worth of opposing positions. We can have hopefully stimulating symposia such as this one. Yet, as a partisan in the controversy, I would prefer unanimous support of the position to which I subscribe. You see, the other people are wrong. Adhering to a philosophic tenet that error is evil, I hate to see my friends wallowing in sin.

Moreover, their particular form of sin is more dangerous than some of the time-honored perversions of civilized societies. For example, it will probably harm more people than the most exotic forms of pornography. I believe that those who discourage educators from precisely explicating their instructional objectives are often permitting, if not promoting, the same kind of unclear thinking that has led in part to the generally abysmal quality of instruction in this country.

In the remainder of this paper I shall examine eleven reasons given by my colleagues in opposition to objectives stated in terms of measurable learner behaviors. I believe each of these reasons is, for the most part, invalid. There may be minor elements of truth in some; after all, the most vile pornographer must occasionally use a few clean words. In essence, however, none of these reasons should be considered strong enough to

*This paper was presented at the annual American Educational Research Association meeting, Chicago, Illinois, February 7–10, 1968. The authors are indebted to Dr. Popham for granting permission to publish the paper in this volume.

deter educators from specifying all of their instructional goals in the precise form advocated by the "good guys" in this argument.

I shall not attempt to develop any arguments in favor of precisely stated goals, for these are treated elsewhere.* My only concern will be with the dubious validity of each of the following reasons.†

Reason one: Trivial learner behaviors are the easiest to operationalize, hence the really important outcomes of education will be under-emphasized.

This particular objection to the use of precise goals is frequently voiced by educators who have recently become acquainted with the procedures for stating explicit, behavioral objectives. Since even behavioral objectives enthusiasts admit that the easiest kinds of pupil behaviors to operationalize are usually the most pedestrian, it is not surprising to find so many examples of behavioral objectives which deal with the picayune. In spite of its overall beneficial influence, the programmed booklet by Robert Mager (1962) dealing with the preparation of instructional objectives has probably suggested to many that precise objectives are usually trivial. Almost all of Mager's examples deal with cognitive behaviors which, according to Bloom's taxonomy, would be identified at the very lowest level.

Contrary to the objection raised in reason one, however, the truth is that explicit objectives make it far *easier* for educators to attend to *important* instructional outcomes. To illustrate, if you were to ask a social science teacher what his objectives were for his government class and he responded as follows, "I want to make my students better citizens so that they can function effectively in our nation's dynamic democracy," you would probably find little reason to fault him. His objective sounds so profound and eminently worthwhile that few could criticize it. Yet, beneath such facades of profundity, many teachers really are aiming at extremely trivial kinds of pupil behavior changes. How often, for example, do we find "good citizenship" measured by a trifling true-false test. Now if we'd asked for the teacher's objectives in operational terms and had discovered that, indeed, all the teacher was attempting to do was promote the learner's achievement on a true-false test, we might have rejected the

---

*W. James Popham, *Educational Objectives.* Los Angeles: Vimcet Associates, 1966; W. James Popham, *Selecting Appropriate Educational Objectives.* Los Angeles: Vimcet Associates, 1967.

†Many of the following remarks are adapted from a symposium presentation at the 19th Annual Conference on Educational Research, California Advisory Council on Educational Research, San Diego, California, November 16, 1967.

aim as being unimportant. But this is possible *only* with the precision of explicitly stated goals.

In other words, there is the danger that because of their ready translation to operational statements, teachers will tend to identify too many trivial behaviors as goals. But the very fact that we can make these behaviors explicit permits the teacher and his colleagues to scrutinize them carefully and thus eliminate them as unworthy of our educational efforts. Instead of encouraging unimportant outcomes in education, the use of explicit instructional objectives makes it possible to identify and reject those objectives which are unimportant.

Reason two: Prespecification of explicit goals prevents the teacher from taking advantage of instructional opportunities unexpectedly occurring in the classroom.

When one specifies explicit *ends* for an instructional program there is no necessary implication that the *means* to achieve those ends are also specified. Serendipity in the classroom is always welcome but, and here is the important point, *it should always be justified in terms of its contribution to the learner's attainment of worthwhile objectives.* Too often teachers may believe they are capitalizing on unexpected instructional opportunities in the classroom, whereas measurement of pupil growth toward any defensible criterion would demonstrate that what has happened is merely ephemeral entertainment for the pupils, temporary diversion, or some other irrelevant classroom event.

Prespecification of explicit goals does not prevent the teacher from taking advantage of unexpectedly occurring instructional opportunities in the classroom; it only tends to make the teacher justify these spontaneous learning activities in terms of worthwhile instructional ends. There are undoubtedly gifted teachers who can capitalize magnificently on the most unexpected classroom events. These teachers should not be restricted from doing so. But the teacher who prefers to probe instructional periphery, just for the sake of its spontaneity, should be deterred by the prespecification of explicit goals.

Reason three: Besides pupil behavior changes, there are other types of educational outcomes which are important, such as changes in parental attitudes, the professional staff, community values, etc.

There are undoubtedly some fairly strong philosophic considerations associated with this particular reason. It seems reasonable that there are desirable changes to be made in our society which might be undertaken by the schools. Certainly, we would like to bring about desirable modifications in such realms as the attitudes of parents. But as a number of educational philosophers have reminded us, the schools cannot be all things to all segments of society. It seems that the primary responsibility of the schools should be to educate effectively the youth of the society. And to the extent that this is so, all modifications of parental attitudes, professional staff attitudes, etc., should be weighed in terms of a later measurable impact on the learner himself. For example, the school administrator who tells us that he wishes to bring about new kinds of attitudes on the part of his teachers should ultimately have to demonstrate that these modified attitudes result in some kind of desirable learner changes. To stop at merely modifying the behavior of teachers, without demonstrating further effects upon the learner, would be insufficient.

So while we can see that there are other types of important social outcomes to bring about, it seems that the school's primary responsibility is to its pupils. Hence, all modifications in personnel or external agencies should be justified in terms of their contribution toward the promotion of desired pupil behavior changes.

Reason four: Measurability implies behavior which can be objectively, mechanistically measured, hence there must be something dehumanizing about the approach.

This fourth reason is drawn from a long history of resistance to measurement on the grounds that it must, of necessity, reduce human learners to quantifiable bits of data. This resistance probably is most strong regarding earlier forms of measurement which were almost exclusively examination-based, and were frequently multiple-choice test measures at that. But a broadened conception of evaluation suggests that there are diverse and extremely sophisticated ways of securing qualitative as well as quantitative indices of learner performance.

One is constantly amazed to note the incredible agreement among a group of judges assigned to evaluate the complicated gyrations of skilled springboard divers in the televised reports of national aquatic championships. One of these athletes will perform an exotic, twisting dive and a few seconds after he has hit the water five or more judges raise cards reflecting their independent evaluations which can range from 0 to 10. The five ratings very frequently run as follows: 7.8, 7.6, 7.7, 7.8, and 7.5. The possibility of reliably judging something as qualitatively complicated as a springboard dive does suggest that our measurement procedures do not have to be based on a theory of reductionism. It is currently possible to assess many complicated human behaviors in a refined fashion. Developmental work is underway in those areas where we now must rely on primitive measures.

Reason five: It is somehow undemocratic to plan in advance precisely how the learner should behave after instruction.

This particular reason was raised a few years ago in a professional journal (Arnstine, 1964) suggesting that the programmed instruction movement was basically undemocratic because it spelled out in advance how the learner was supposed to behave after instruction. A brilliant refutation (Komisar and McClellan, 1965) appeared several months later in which the rebutting authors responded that instruction is by its very nature undemocratic and to imply that freewheeling democracy is always present in the classroom would be untruthful. Teachers generally have an idea of how they wish learners to behave, and they promote these goals with more or less efficiency. Society knows what it wants its young to become, perhaps not with the precision that we would desire, but certainly in general. And if the schools were allowing students to "democratically" deviate from societally-mandated goals, one can be sure that the institutions would cease to receive society's approbation and support.

Reason six: That isn't really the way teaching is; teachers rarely specify their goals in terms of measurable learner behaviors; so let's set realistic expectations of teachers.

Jackson (1966) recently offered this argument. He observed that teachers just don't specify their objectives in terms of measurable learner behavior and implied that, since this is the way the real world is, we ought to recognize it and live with it. Perhaps.

There is obviously a difference between identifying the status quo and applauding it. Most of us would readily concede that few teachers specify their instructional aims in terms of measurable learner behaviors, *but they ought to.* What we have to do is to mount a widespread campaign to modify this aspect of teacher behavior. Instructors must begin to identify their instructional intentions in terms of measurable learner behaviors. The way teaching really is at the moment just isn't good enough.

Reason seven: In certain subject areas, e.g., fine arts and the humanities, it is more difficult to identify measurable pupil behaviors.

Sure it's tough. Yet, because it is difficult in certain subject fields to identify measurable pupil behaviors, those subject specialists should not be allowed to escape this responsibility. Teachers in the fields of art and music often claim that it is next to impossible to identify acceptable works of art in precise terms—but they do it all the time. In instance after instance the art teacher does make a judgment regarding the acceptability of pupil-produced artwork. What the art teacher is reluctant to do is put his evaluative criteria on the line. He has such criteria. He must have to make his judgments. But he is loath to describe them in terms that anyone can see.

Any English teacher, for example, will tell you how difficult it is to make a valid judgment of a pupil's essay response. Yet criteria lurk whenever this teacher does make a judgment, and these criteria must be made explicit. No one who really understands education has ever argued that instruction is a simple task. It is even more difficult in such areas as the arts and humanities. As a noted art educator observed several years ago, art educators must quickly get to the business of specifying "tentative, but clearly defined criteria" by which they can judge their learners' artistic efforts (Munro, 1960).

Reason eight: While loose general statements of objectives may appear worthwhile to an outsider, if most educational goals were stated precisely, they would be revealed as generally innocuous.

This eighth reason contains a great deal of potential threat for school people. The unfortunate truth is that much of what is going on in the schools today is indefensible. Merely to reveal the nature of some behavior changes we are bringing about in our schools would be embarrassing. As long as general objectives are the rule, our goals may appear worthwhile to external observers. But once we start to describe precisely what kinds of changes we are bringing about in the learner, there is the danger that the public will reject our intentions as unworthy. Yet, if what we are doing is trivial, educators would know it and those who support the educational institution should also know it. To the extent that we are achieving innocuous behavior changes in learners, we are guilty. We must abandon the ploy of "obfuscation by generality" and make clear exactly what we are doing. Then we are obliged to defend our choices.

Reason nine: Measurability implies accountability; teachers might be judged on their ability to produce results in learners rather than on the many bases now used as indices of competence.

This is a particularly threatening reason and serves to produce much teacher resistance to precisely stated objectives. It doesn't take too much insight on the part of the teacher to realize that if objectives are specified in terms of measurable learner behavior, there exists the possibility that the instructor will have to become *accountable* for securing such behavior changes. Teachers might actually be judged on their ability to bring about desirable changes in learners. They should be.

But a teacher should not be judged on the particular instructional *means* he uses to bring about desirable *ends*. At present many teachers are judged adversely simply because the instructional procedures they use do not coincide with those once used by an evaluator when "he was a teacher." In other words, if I'm a supervisor who has had considerable success with open-ended discussion, I may tend to view with disfavor any teachers who cleave to more directive methods. Yet, if the teacher using the more direct methods can secure learner behavior changes which are desirable, I have no right to judge that teacher as inadequate. The possibility of assessing instructional competence in terms of the teacher's ability to bring about specified behavior changes in learners brings with it far more assets than liabilities to the teacher. He will no longer be judged on the idiosyncratic whims of a visiting supervisor. Rather, he can amass evidence that, in terms of his pupils' actual attainments, he is able to teach efficiently.

Even though this is a striking departure from the current state of affairs, and a departure that may be threatening to the less competent, the educator must promote this kind of accountability rather than the maze of folklore and mysticism which exists at the moment regarding teacher evaluation.

Reason ten: It is far more difficult to generate such precise objectives than to talk about objectives in our customarily vague terms.

Here is a very significant objection to the development of precise goals. Teachers are, for the most part, far too busy to spend the necessary hours in stating their objectives and measurement procedures with the kind of precision implied by this discussion. It is said that we are soon nearing a time when we will have more teachers than jobs. This is the time to reduce the teacher's load to the point where he can become a professional decision-maker rather than a custodian. We must reduce public school teaching loads to those of college professors. This is the time when we must give the teacher immense help in specifying his objectives. Perhaps we should *give* him objectives from which to choose, rather than force him to generate his own. Many of the federal dollars currently being used to support education would be better spent on agencies which would produce alternative behavioral objectives for all fields at all grade levels. At any rate, the difficulty of the task should not preclude its accomplishment. We can recognize how hard the job is and still allocate the necessary resources to do it.

Reason eleven: In evaluating the worth of instructional schemes it is often the unanticipated results which are really important, but prespecified goals may make the evaluator inattentive to the unforeseen.
Some fear that if we cleave to behaviorally stated objectives which must be specified prior to designing an instructional program, we will overlook certain outcomes of the program which were not anticipated yet which may be extremely important. They point out that some of the relatively recent "new curricula" in the sciences have had the unanticipated effect of sharply reducing pupil enrollments in those fields. In view of the possibility of such outcomes, both unexpectedly good and bad, it is suggested that we really ought not spell out objectives in advance, but should evaluate the adequacy of the instructional program after it has been implemented.

Such reasoning, while compelling at first glance, weakens under close scrutiny. In the first place, really dramatic unanticipated outcomes cannot be overlooked by curriculum evaluators. They certainly should not be. We should judge an instructional sequence not only by whether it attains its prespecified objectives, but also by any unforeseen consequences it produces. But what can you tell the would-be curriculum evaluator regarding this problem? "Keep your eyes open," doesn't seem to pack the desired punch. Yet, it's about all you can say. For if there is reason to believe that a particular outcome may result from an instructional sequence, it should be built into the set of objectives for the sequence. To illustrate, if the curriculum designers fear that certain negative attitudes will be acquired by the learner as he interacts with an instructional sequence, then behavioral objectives can be devised which reveal whether the instructional sequence has effectively counteracted this affective outcome. It is probably always a good idea, for example, to identify behavioral indices of the pupil's "subject-approaching tendencies." We don't want to teach youngsters how to perform mathematical exercises, for example, but to learn to hate math in the process.

Yet, it is indefensible to let an awareness of the importance of unanticipated outcomes in evaluating instructional programs lead one to the rejection of rigorous pre-planning of instructional objectives. Such objectives should be the primary, but not exclusive, focus in evaluating instruction.

While these eleven reasons are not exhaustive, they represent most of the arguments used to resist the implementation of precise instructional objectives. In spite of the very favorable overall reaction to explicit objectives during the past five to ten years, a small collection of dissident educators has arisen to oppose the quest for goal specificity. The trouble with criticisms of precise objectives isn't that they are completely without foundation. As conceded earlier, there are probably elements of truth in all of them. Yet, when we are attempting to promote the wide-scale adoption of precision in the classroom, there is the danger that many instructors will use the comments and objections of these few critics as an excuse from thinking clearly about their goals. Any risks we run by moving to behavioral goals are miniscule in contrast with our current state of confusion regarding instructional intentions. The objections against behaviorally stated goals are not strong enough. To secure a dramatic increase in instructional effectiveness we must abandon our customary practices of goal-stating and turn to a framework of precision.

References

Arnstine, D. G. (1964), The language and values of programmed instruction: part 2. *The Educational Forum, 28.*

Jackson, P. W. (1966), *The way teaching is.* Washington, D. C.: National Education Association.

Komisar, P. B., & McClellan, J. E. (1965), Professor Arnstine and programmed instruction. Reprint from *The Educational Forum.*

Mager, R. F. (1962), *Preparing instructional objectives.* San Francisco: Fearon Publishers.

Munro, T. (1960), The interrelation of the arts in secondary education. In *The creative arts in American education.* Cambridge, Mass.: Harvard University Press.

Below are three additional issues concerning the use of instructional objectives that Dr. Popham does not discuss in his paper (Kibler, Barker, and Miles, 1970; Kibler, Barker, and Cegala, 1970a).

1. Prespecifying the Objectives for a Unit of Instruction That a Teacher Has Not Previously Taught. This is indeed a complex task. But it has been our experience that a procedure such as the following can reduce some of the complexity and result in a fairly complete set of objectives for the succeeding times the course is taught.

A. Specify a set of objectives, stating them in general terms. These objectives should be based on an analysis of postinstructional performance expectancies and preinstructional performance capabilities.
B. Specify more precise objectives for each unit as it occurs.
C. Evaluate the results of each unit, and base the objectives for the following units on these results.
D. Identify and record objectives which are achieved in addition to those prespecified for each unit.

This procedure is essentially a crude technique for testing hypotheses regarding objectives, identifying unpredicted objectives, and determining criteria for appropriate levels of performance. Thus, experience with the first attempt at a course is used to develop a set of precise objectives for succeeding presentations of the course.

2. Deciding Whether All Students Should Be Required to Achieve the Same Objectives. With the increasing emphasis on individualized instruction, this decision is indeed relevant. Our viewpoint is that for most courses in public school, industrial, and undergraduate education, all students should achieve a common set of goals. This does not, however, preclude the possibility of specification of instructional objectives for *individual* student achievement. Opportunities should be available for students in many of these courses to go beyond the basic requirements to pursue individual areas of interest. One technique that has been employed frequently involves each student's stating his/her specific objectives. Such a procedure seems quite appropriate when one of the teacher's objectives is for students to be able to identify and acquire behavioral competencies of personal concern.

3. Deciding Whether All Students Should Be Required to Achieve the Same Level of Mastery for Each Objective. This issue is related to the previous one. Brought into question here is the value of using the norm-referenced evaluation and grading system, in which students are assessed on the basis of their performance relative to the group, instead of the criterion-referenced system, in which students are evaluated according to their achievement of specified criteria—irrespective of how the group performs. The norm-referenced system is presently the most widely used system, although the criterion-referenced system is growing in popularity. (Further discussion of these systems is presented in chapter 6.)

Without clearly defined objectives and performance criteria for measuring attainment of the objectives, the norm-referenced system is probably the most reasonable method available for assessing student achievement. However, given specific objectives and evaluation criteria, the practice of measuring the relative achievement of the objective may be open to question. Much has been written on this issue recently, and very likely the increased use of instructional objectives is to a great extent responsible for the dialogue.

Some educators feel that the purpose of education is not to determine who learns more and less of a given subject matter, but rather to see to it that all students learn what is considered necessary. From this viewpoint, the criterion-referenced system would be the desirable choice, and all students could be required to achieve the same level of mastery on each objective. This approach does not negate the possibility of providing the opportunity for students to go beyond the basic required objectives. The latter possibility may be extremely important to a more widespread acceptance of criterion-referenced evaluation, since the relative achievement information (presently provided by norm-referenced evaluation and grading) is employed for a large variety of seemingly vital functions. School grades are used as a basis for selecting students for college, major areas of study, graduate school, honors programs, scholarships, and post-school employment; for retaining students in school; for influencing students' occupational choices; and for recording progress toward certificates and degrees. They also are used as incentives and rewards. Thus, it appears that some kind of information regarding a student's academic performance relative to other students is needed. Possibly standardized academic ability or achievement tests eventually can provide such information and the results of instructional evaluation could be used only for determining the effectiveness of instruction when students have achieved specified objectives.

Two generalizations regarding this issue seem appropriate. When mastery of an objective is vital to the achievement of subsequent objectives (for example, some language and computational skills are essential to much of what follows in and comes after school), then all students should be required to master the objective fully. When subsequent performance demands are not so clear-cut, it may be appropriate to permit students to achieve varying levels of mastery of an objective—above some minimum criterion.

The other generalization involves the domain of evaluation in education. The three primary functions of evaluation in instruction are to provide information regarding (1) student achievement of instructional objectives; (2) the success of instruction in getting students to achieve objectives; and (3) student achievement and ability that can be used for academic and occupational selection. Although both the norm-referenced and criterion-referenced systems can provide information for the three functions, the criterion-referenced system probably is a more desirable procedure for accomplishing the first and second functions, and the norm-referenced system is more appropriate for meeting the third function. The different amounts of time students spend in reaching criteria could provide information for function 3 within a criterion-referenced system, but such a practice may tend to result in an overemphasis on speed of acquisition and an underemphasis on retention and transfer.

Thus, it is our position that a criterion-referenced system should be employed for the basic fundamentals of instruction, and all students should be required to meet the standards considered necessary for post-instruction performance. In addition, opportunities for students to go beyond the required standards should be provided, and the results of students' performance in these areas, plus the results of standardized achievement and ability tests, should be used to satisfy the functions for which grades are used presently.

In the first part of this chapter we have attempted to present several reasons for using instructional objectives. Even so, we do not expect all of our readers to become instant converts. Those who remain skeptical may find the rest of this book frustrating, as it focuses on the use of instructional objectives and how their implementation relates to other key components of the instructional process.

THE GENERAL MODEL OF INSTRUCTION

We have just examined several key issues in the current controversy over the use of instructional objectives. It is our belief that much of the confusion and controversy about the use of instructional objectives stems from a lack of information that systematically integrates instructional objectives with other key components of the instructional process. Accordingly, we have organized our examination of instructional objectives in a manner designed to illustrate (1) how objectives relate to key components of the instructional process, (2) the implications for teachers and students when instruction incorporates objectives, and (3) how objectives may be used to improve instruction throughout various stages of the entire instructional process. To provide coherency in meeting these goals, we have devoted subsequent chapters of this book to a discussion of instructional objectives as they relate to various components of a general model of instruction.

The general model of instruction is a procedural guide for the design, implementation, evaluation, and improvement of instruction. The model is applicable to all levels of education (e.g., elementary, secondary, higher), all subject matters (e.g., English, science, art, vocational), and any length of instructional unit (e.g., one hour, one week, one semester).

The major premise underlying the model is that the goal of teaching is to maximize the efficiency/effectiveness and minimize the anxiety with which students achieve specified objectives. More specific assumptions of the model are that *most effective* instruction occurs when:

1. Maximum communication exists between teacher and learner regarding the objectives and goals of instruction;
2. Learners are provided with instructional objectives tailored to individual needs and capabilities;
3. Learners are provided with instructional experiences that are designed to help them achieve goals stated in instructional objectives;
4. Learners are given the opportunity to progress and, if need be, to recycle through instructional units at their own pace until mastery of instructional objectives is achieved.

Even if it is not possible for instruction to reflect all of these assumptions, the general model of instruction can be used effectively to guide instructional designers and teachers through the major steps in designing and carrying out instruction, and to provide an overall structure with which to view and study the instructional process.

The general model of instruction does not propose to tell teachers what they should teach or what specific instructional methods they should employ. The general model of instruction presents a guide for the teacher to use in deciding (1) what he/she would like students to learn, (2) what instructional methods he/she would employ, and (3) how to determine whether students learned what was intended. The range of possible objectives from which a teacher can select is nearly limitless. There are dozens of different methods of teaching, and each teacher generally employs each method somewhat differently. A wide variety of equally valid means of evaluation also exists. Each individual teacher must make decisions regarding objectives, instructional procedures, and evaluation on the basis of several factors, such as (1) personal views of what is important for students to learn, (2) the community and institution in which he/she teaches, (3) the type of students he/she has, and (4) his/her preferences and capabilities regarding instructional methods and resources. The general model of instruction is primarily concerned with helping teachers teach what, and how, they want to teach as well as possible.

Although the model itself has not been validated experimentally for instructional efficiency, several of the prescriptive principles contained in it are derived from empirical research. The model is based on a technology of instruction that has been developed in the past several years from the research and development work in three areas—experimental psychology, military training, and programed instruction. The four individuals who have contributed most to the specific model presented in this document are Robert Gagné (1965a, 1965b, and 1970), Robert Glaser (1965), W. James Popham (1965), and Ralph W. Tyler (1950).

A flow diagram of the model is shown. Each step in the model actually composes a body of knowledge with which anyone concerned with instruction should be intimately familiar.

On the following pages each component of the model is explained briefly, and several of the major factors to consider at each step in the model are presented. The material is designed to provide an overview of the instructional process. In subsequent chapters each component of the model is discussed more fully, particularly as each relates to the use of instructional objectives.

Instructional Objectives

Preparing instructional objectives is probably the most important step in the entire model, for the instructor must decide what he/she wants to teach. The four major factors involved in preparing objectives—selection, classification, analysis, and specification—are discussed briefly below.

Selection. The selection of appropriate objectives usually is based on the following factors: (1) what the students are able to do before beginning the unit; (2) what the students should be able to do in instructional units that follow the unit of concern and what they should be able to do after completing their education; and (3) the available instructional resources, including the instructor's capabilities with his/her subject matter.

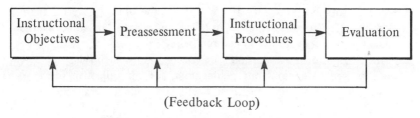

(Feedback Loop)

FIGURE 1. A General Model of Instruction

Classification. The taxonomies, by Bloom and others (1956) and Krathwohl and others (1964), are useful in making sure that the objectives selected are of the level or type actually desired. For example, by classifying objectives in the cognitive domain into taxonomic categories, the instructor can determine whether the desired behaviors are knowledge, comprehension, application, analysis, synthesis, or evaluation. Gagné (1970) and Guilford (1967) also have produced systems for classifying human performance that are useful for this purpose.

Analysis. Once a set of objectives has been selected, the instructor should perform a behavioral analysis in which he/she determines what a student will be expected to *do* to demonstrate achievement of the objective. The actual components to be examined in a behavioral analysis are (1) the important stimuli to which a student responds; (2) the important responses made; and (3) the criteria which the responses must meet to be considered successful.

Such an analysis can be performed by observing students who have already achieved the objective as they exhibit the desired behavior. Previous students can be interviewed, and the products (tests, papers, etc.) they produced can be examined. No matter how the behavioral analysis is conducted, a list should be compiled of the instructional objectives that clearly and completely prescribe the behaviors students are to acquire as a result of completing the instruction.

Specification. Instructional objectives will be most valuable if they contain the following three elements recommended by Robert Mager in *Preparing Instructional Objectives* (1962):

1. A description of the type of *observable behavior* that the student will be asked to employ in demonstrating mastery of the objective (e.g., "to

write," "to solve," "to identify," "to describe orally"). Terms such as "to know," "to understand," and "to appreciate" must be avoided, since they do not refer to observable behavior.

2. A description of the important *conditions* under which the student will be expected to demonstrate achievement of the objective (e.g., time limits, materials or equipment that will be available, or special instructions).

3. The *criterion* that will be used to evaluate the success of the student's performance (e.g., must get 70 percent correct, correctly apply three principles, complete the task in fifteen minutes, or correctly identify eight out of ten).

Prior to moving on, it should be emphasized that the function of these instructional objectives is for *planning* instruction, not for *informing* others of instructional intentions. These objectives are more detailed than the objectives used typically for the purpose of communicating goals to others. Several types of extremely important objectives are difficult to measure and, thus, difficult to specify in behavioral terms. As a matter of fact, it seems that the more significant an objective is, the more difficult it is to measure. Examples of objectives which fall into the difficult-to-specify-and-measure category are those in the areas of problem solving, creativity, attitudes, and values. The only solution we see to this problem is for such objectives to be specified as clearly as possible and for the instructor to be as resourceful as he/she can be in developing evaluative measures, including attitude inventories and creativity tests.

Such objectives (e.g., "to shape favorable attitudes toward your subject matter and toward learning") should *not* be eliminated because they are difficult to measure; they should be included, and the instructor should work toward improving his/her measures. We have included samples of some of these types of objectives in Appendix A.

Preassessment

Prior to beginning a unit of instruction, it is desirable to assess students to determine (1) how much of what is to be learned in the unit they already know; (2) whether they have the necessary behavioral capabilities for the instruction to follow; and (3) the instructional activities that should be prescribed for each student. Of course, the assessment should be based on the specific instructional objectives designated for the unit. The results of this assessment should indicate (1) whether any students may *omit* any of the objectives in the unit; (2) whether any students should be required to master *prerequisite* skills before beginning the unit; and (3) what specific *instructional activities* should be provided for specific students. The above alternative courses of action imply that individualized instruction or tracking procedures are available for the instructional event. However, it is frequently possible to require prerequisite behavioral competencies and omit objectives for individual students in group-paced instruction.

Instructional Procedures

After students are preassessed and adjustments are made, such as adding or eliminating objectives or requiring prerequisite learning, the instructional procedures are implemented. The design of the instructional procedures involves (1) selecting available instructional materials (e.g., books, films, or lesson plan); (2) preparing new instructional materials when necessary; and (3) developing a sequential plan that appears to be the most efficient for achieving the stated objectives. Decisions should be based upon research evidence when it is available.

Evaluation

When students complete an instructional unit, they are evaluated to determine whether the instruction was successful in achieving the unit's objectives. Typically, evaluation involves using tests and instruments to measure the acquisition of knowledge, skills, and attitudes. Frequently, it is necessary to specify or describe student achievement. This is usually a difficult task.

If the objectives have been specified clearly, test preparation is made easier. (We are not suggesting, however, that test construction is made easy.) An important consideration in designing evaluative measures is that the instrument measure the identical behavior specified in the objectives. It also is important to note that the success of the instruction, as well as the success of the students, is evaluated.

In most instances in formal education, it is both desirable and feasible for almost all (if not *all*) students to master almost all (if not *all*) objectives. If individual students do not perform acceptably on all objectives, an explanation must be sought from among the following three reasons:

1. The unsuccessful students were prepared inadequately for the unit, which could mean that the objectives were unrealistic or that the students should not have begun the unit without prior training.
2. The unsuccessful students were not motivated properly to master the material.
3. The instruction was not designed properly, or insufficient time was provided for the students to master the objectives.

Changes in the objectives, the preinstruction procedures, the instruction, or the postinstruction evaluation are to be made on the basis of the evaluational results (note the *feedback loop* on the flow chart). In addition to making changes based on observed results, instructors should make modifications on the basis of new developments in materials and techniques, new research findings, and changing values.

The results of evaluation also can be used to inform students and other interested parties about the degree of success each student achieved in the unit. However, since all students may be required to master all objectives, this information may consist of only an indication of the different lengths of time each student took to complete the unit.

The most important factors you should remember about evaluation are these:

1. It is the success of the *instruction,* as well as the success of students, that is being evaluated.
2. Unsuccessful instruction is probably a result of one of the following:
   a. Students did not have the *prerequisites* necessary to begin the unit;
   b. The students were *motivated inadequately* before or during the unit;
   c. The instructional activities were *designed inadequately;*
   d. The objectives were too difficult for students;
   e. The measurement process may have been inadequate.
3. Changes in objectives, preassessment, and instructional procedures should be made, if necessary, so that ideally all students achieve all required objectives.

Feedback Loop

The feedback loop in the model serves two purposes. As already indicated, the feedback loop serves to remind teachers that the results of evaluation may indicate that other components of the instructional process (e.g., objectives, preassessment procedures, instructional procedures) need modification. Another purpose of the feedback loop is concerned with the issue of providing students with feedback about their progress in learning. Ammons' (1956) exhaustive review of the literature on the effects of knowledge of performance suggests that students learn more rapidly and reach higher levels of performance when provided with knowledge of performance. Recent research reported by Bloom, Hastings, and Madaus (1971) on formative and summative evaluation procedures also supports Ammons' generalization. Moreover, Airasian (1971) and Duchastel and Merrill (1973) have suggested that instructional objectives may facilitate learning by providing feedback concerning student progress. For example, Airasian (1971) has suggested that upon completion of a formative test,[2] a student should be provided with immediate feedback of the objectives corresponding to the test items that the student answered correctly. By identifying unmastered objectives, the student may then direct his/her energies to corrective activities that may enable him/her to overcome deficiencies in performance. Of course, such a strategy assumes that the student is provided with instructional objectives and multiple test attempts and that he/she is encouraged to work toward predetermined mastery levels. We will discuss the concepts of multiple testing procedures and mastery learning more fully in chapter 6.

SUMMARY

In the first part of the chapter a rationale for instructional objectives and their use was presented. The rationale reflected three perspectives on reasons for using instructional objectives: a rational perspective, an empirical perspective, and a functional perspective. Under the rational perspective several reasons were offered, on logical grounds, for using instructional objectives. The empirical perspective included a review of experimental research concerned with the effects of instructional objectives on student learning. It was emphasized that the research findings to date are inconsistent and offer no conclusive generalizations about the effects of instructional objectives on student achievement. Consequently, a third view, the functional perspective, was examined in an attempt to resolve some of the

---

[2]A formative test is given during the course of instruction for feedback purposes. It is not a test of terminal performance.

controversy over instructional objectives and their use. Under the functional perspective several key issues concerning the use of instructional objectives were described and examined.

The second part of the chapter focused on the general model of instruction. Each component of the model was described briefly and related to the use of instructional objectives. A synthesis of the key components and concepts of the model is presented below:

Premise of the model: The goal of teaching is to maximize the efficiency/effectiveness and minimize the anxiety with which students achieve specified objectives.

Functions of the model: (1) to guide instruction design and implementation; (2) to provide structure for viewing and studying instruction.

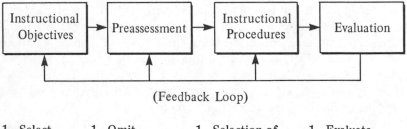

(Feedback Loop)

1. Select	1. Omit objectives	1. Selection of available materials	1. Evaluate instruction
2. Classify	2. Require prerequisites	2. Preparing new materials	2. Cause of failure (a) prerequisite (b) motivation (c) instruction (d) objectives (e) measurement
3. Analyze	3. Prescribe instruction	3. Developing a sequential plan	3. Modify to achieve 100% (or near) mastery
4. Specify			

(1) Use feedback information to make needed modifications in other components of the model.

(2) Provide learners with knowledge of performance throughout instruction.

2

INSTRUCTIONAL OBJECTIVES

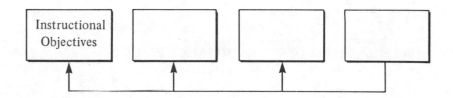

After completing this chapter, the learner should be able to:

1. Define a general objective and provide an example of a general educational objective;
2. Compare general objectives and instructional objectives in terms of specificity and purpose;
3. Define the terms *behavior* and *performance* as they apply to instructional objectives;
4. Identify and define five components of instructional objectives;
5. List and define ten action verbs that may be used in writing instructional objectives;
6. Describe three ways to determine what relevant conditions should be specified in an instructional objective;
7. Define *performance standard* and provide examples of different classes of performance standards;
8. Distinguish between performance standards that pertain to minimal level of mastery and performance standards that pertain to accuracy of performance.

In this chapter we will focus our attention on the first component of the general model of instruction—instructional objectives. First, the nature and function of instructional objectives is examined by distinguishing instructional objectives from other types of educational objectives. Second, three options are offered to you for learning how to write instructional objectives: (1) a textual reading option, where each component of instructional objectives is described and illustrated, (2) a programed text option, where components of instructional objectives are described and illustrated, and opportunity for practice and immediate feedback is provided, and (3) a combination option, where both the first and second options are taken. The chapter concludes with a discussion of selected difficulties encountered in specifying instructional objectives and with suggestions for reducing and/or eliminating these difficulties.

DIFFERENT TYPES OF EDUCATIONAL OBJECTIVES

Educational objectives are written at various levels of specificity and for different purposes. Figure 2 shows how objectives differ with respect to specificity and purpose.

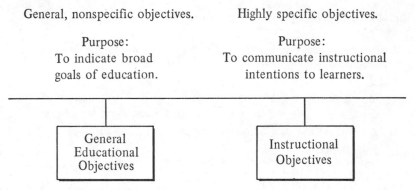

General, nonspecific objectives.   Highly specific objectives.

Purpose: Purpose:
To indicate broad   To communicate instructional
goals of education.   intentions to learners.

| General Educational Objectives | | Instructional Objectives |

FIGURE 2. Specificity/Purpose Continuum of Objectives

At the extreme end of nonspecificity are the very general objectives of educational institutions and broad educational programs. Most readers have been exposed to these types of objectives, which are called *general educational objectives.* A discussion of general educational objectives is included in *The Cardinal Principles of Secondary Education* (1937) and, more recently, in *The Central Purposes of American Education* (1961), published by the Educational Policies Commission of the National Education Association. Examples of general educational objectives are "to make better citizens," "to advance humanity," and "to promote our cultural ideals." General objectives are important in the educational process because they relate the broad goals of education to the needs and expectations of society. General objectives often provide the philosophical guidance necessary for determining what specific instructional objectives ought to be included in a given curriculum. Even so, not all (but certainly some) general objectives have a one-to-one correspondence with instructional objectives for a given curriculum, since general objectives typically refer to the broad future goals that educators hope to achieve. This is not to say that instructional objectives have no relationship to future goals; rather it is to say that often several instructional objectives in a given curriculum relate to one broad future goal that educators hope to achieve. Moreover, a reasonably large portion of general objectives typically refers to affective goals that often are not easily amenable to specification of learner development in observable, measurable terms.

At the other end of the educational objective continuum are specific instructional objectives—that type of instructional objective on which the general model of instruction presented in chapter 1 focuses. Instructional objectives require specification of student learning in terms of observable, measurable behavior. An example of this type of instructional objective is:

> In a half-hour test at the end of the week, the student will be able to list the steps a bill follows through Congress, specifying the requirements for passage at each step. All steps must be included in the correct order, and the passage requirements must match the ones in the textbook.

Some educational objectives do not fit neatly into either the general or instructional objective category—such examples include outlines of objectives for elementary (Kearney, 1953) and secondary (French, 1957) educational levels, some objectives that have been developed for the language arts (Lazarus and Knudson, 1967), and the types of objectives included in the two volumes of the *Taxonomy of Educational Objectives* (Bloom et al., 1956, and Krathwohl et al., 1964). These objectives would be placed at varying points between general educational objectives and instructional objectives.

In particular, many (but not all) affective educational goals are appropriately placed between the general objective and instructional objective categories. Because of their dependence on the specification of observable measurable behavior, instructional objectives most often are prepared for the cognitive and psychomotor domains. This is not to say that instructional objectives cannot be prepared for the affective domain, but many important affective objectives simply do not lend themselves to the type of specification illustrated by the instructional objective on page 31. Consequently, many affective (and some cognitive and psychomotor) objectives fall somewhere between general and instructional objectives and are used for a variety of purposes, including communicating instructional intentions to students and other teachers. Examples of these appear below:

1. The student seeks and reads books that are considered literary masterpieces.
2. The student watches educational television at home.
3. The student participates in extracurricular activities related to science class.
4. The student demonstrates a willingness to accept criticism from peers.
5. The student willingly complies to rules governing socially acceptable behavior in a variety of situations.
6. The student is able to discriminate various moods and meanings of classical music and explain his/her interpretations to others.

WRITING INSTRUCTIONAL OBJECTIVES

Most educational objectives, specific or otherwise, serve a valuable function in the educational process. The general model of instruction presented in chapter 1 primarily focuses on the role and function of the more specific type of instructional objective, although less specific objectives also can be used within the model. However, to use the model most effectively, one must acquire the skills necessary to write instructional objectives for his/her content area.

Basic Concepts for Writing Instructional Objectives

This section contains a behavioral analysis of what a student is expected to be able to do when he/she has successfully completed a unit of

---

BRANCHING OPTION TWO

At this point in the chapter we offer you three options for acquiring the skills necessary for writing effective instructional objectives. One option is for you to read carefully the section below entitled "Basic Concepts of Writing Instructional Objectives." This option is designed for those of you who prefer to read about the procedures for writing instructional objectives in a standard textbook format. To benefit maximally from this option, you should have the ability to read and assimilate concepts and subsequently to apply what you have read. In the text below, each component of an instructional objective is defined, discussed, and illustrated. A second option is for you to turn to page 42 and complete the program designed to teach you the components of instructional objectives and to provide you with examples of objectives, practice at writing objectives, and immediate feedback regarding the correctness of your responses. A third option is available; that is, of course, completing both of the first two options. We suggest that you select the third option for maximum learning.

---

instruction. Other authors have used terms like *task description* or *task analysis* to describe similar information (Miller, 1962a, 1962b; Stolurow, 1963; Gagné, 1965a, 1965b, 1970; Taber, Glaser, and Schaefer, 1965; Lange, 1967; and Tyler, Gagné, and Scriven, 1967). By *behavioral analysis* we mean a study of the final behavior to be required of the student broken down into its component parts. Before we examine each of the five parts of this final behavior, it may be valuable to review a few terms and concepts that will be used throughout this volume.

By *behavior* we mean actions and movements that people can be observed (seen, heard, or felt) making. Thus, thinking, which involves electrochemical activity in the brain, is not considered behavior here, since the activity cannot be observed directly with the unaided senses. (However, such activity can be observed indirectly with mechanical devices such as an electroencephalograph.) Therefore, since instructional objectives must identify the action a person must perform, all instructional objectives require a psychomotor component.

Caution must be exercised, however, to avoid overemphasizing the "action" component of objectives; cognitive and affective objectives are concerned with characteristics of thinking and feeling that are themselves not directly observable. States of affection and acts of cognition are inferred from psychomotor acts. We do not see a person analyze a poem; we see or hear a report of his/her analysis. We do not see the mental activity of problem solving; we see tentative solutions to the problem. We do not see the emotional feelings a person experiences when listening to a favorite piece of music; we see the results of his/her emotional experience in his/her verbal response or facial expression or in his/her future selection of that music to which he/she listens.

Actually, we are usually more interested in the characteristics of the products or actions that permit us to infer the type of mental activity that produced them than we are in the form of behavior that made them observable. However, since the only way we can be sure of what happens "inside" people's heads or "hearts" is to look at what they do, we emphasize the observable actions. Objective evidence is required to determine whether a person has thought or felt in a particular way. If instructors were not concerned with making changes in students, they would not have to bother looking at behavior—but they do have that responsibility.

Performance is used in this book to refer to the result of a person's action that is evaluated to see whether he/she has successfully completed an objective. For example, if an objective is for a student to build an electric motor that runs, the "performance" that is evaluated is whether the electric motor runs. Or, if an objective is to write a term paper according to a set of prescribed specifications, the term paper that the student turns in is what is evaluated and thus is considered his/her performance. *Product* is frequently used as a synonym for *performance.*

You will see that these distinctions are necessary as we examine the components of instructional objectives. Gagné (1965a, 1965b, and 1970) has emphasized the importance of understanding the relationship between education and human performance. Human performance must be employed to determine what is *intended* to occur in education. It is also tied into an understanding of learning, since we infer that learning has taken place as a result of observing a change in performance. For example, suppose we observed two performance events separated by a few days. In the first event the student was presented with five sentences and was told to underline the verb in each of them; he/she subsequently failed to perform the task satisfactorily. During the second event a similar set of instructions and list of sentences were presented to the same student. This time the student performed the task successfully. A *change* in the student's performance was observed, which might give us some basis for inferring that the student learned to underline verbs.

Now that some of these basic terms have been reviewed, we will analyze the component parts of the final performance that the student is expected to demonstrate as a result of completing an instructional unit. Instructional objectives should contain the following five elements:

1. *Who* is to perform the desired behavior (e.g., "the student" or "the learner").
2. The *actual behavior* to be employed in demonstrating mastery of the objective (e.g., "to write" or "to speak").
3. The *result* (i.e., the product or performance) of the behavior, which will be evaluated to determine whether the objective is mastered (e.g., "an essay" or "the speech").
4. The *relevant conditions* under which the behavior is to be performed (e.g., "in a one-hour quiz" or "in front of the class").
5. The *standard* that will be used to evaluate the success of the product or performance (e.g., "90 percent correct" or "four out of five correct").

Each of these components is identified in the objective shown below. The number of each *component* is *identified above* the appropriate portion of the instructional objective. Those words and phrases that are not a part of a specific component have no identification appearing above them.

                                            4   1

| During the one-hour mid-term examination, | | the student | | will be

    2   5   3

able | | to spell correctly | | 45 out of 50 | | words | | randomly selected

      4

from the 200 words listed in Units one and two of the spelling book. | |

  1   2   3   4

The student | | will write | | the words | as they are presented orally by the

              5

teacher. | | In order to be correct, the spelling of each word must match

the spelling in the spelling book. |

Who Is to Perform the Desired Behavior. Determining the first component, the *who,* is easy. Obviously, you usually want the *student* to demonstrate the behavior. Other terms for those who may be asked to perform the desired behavior are *learner, pupil,* and *enrollees.*

The Actual Behavior to Be Employed. The second component of an instructional objective is the specific observable act or behavior that the learner is to perform. For example, the student may be instructed "to write," "to identify," or "to distinguish." Researchers working in task analysis have reported a necessity for "hard," "clear" *action verbs* to classify the behavior to be performed (Miller, 1962a and 1962b; Chenzoff and Folley, Jr., 1965). Some of the action words used as operational guides are defined in the following list.

Definitions of Action Words[1]

1. *Identifying.* The individual selects (by pointing to, touching, or picking up) the correct object of a class name. For example: Upon being asked, "Which animal is the frog?" when presented with a set of small animals, the child is expected to respond by picking up or clearly pointing to or touching the frog; if the child is asked to "pick up the red triangle" when presented with a set of paper cutouts representing different shapes, he is expected to pick up the red triangle. This class of performances also includes identifying object properties (such as rough, smooth, straight, curved) and, in addition, kinds of changes such as an increase or decrease in size.

2. *Distinguishing.* Identifying objects or events which are potentially confusable (square, rectangle), or when two contrasting identifications (such as right, left) are involved.

3. *Constructing.* Generating a construction or drawing which identifies a designated object or set of conditions. Example: Beginning with a line segment, the request is made, "Complete this figure so that it represents a triangle."

4. *Naming.* Supplying the correct name (orally or in written form) for a class of objects or events. Example: "What is this three-dimensional object called?" Response: "A cone."

5. *Ordering.* Arranging two or more objects or events in proper order in accordance with a stated category. For example: "Arrange these moving objects in order of their speeds."

6. *Describing.* Generating and naming all of the necessary categories of objects, object properties, or event properties that are relevant to the description of a designated situation. Example: "Describe this object," and the observer does not limit the categories which may be generated by mentioning them, as in the question, "Describe the color

[1]Henry H. Walbesser, *Constructing Behavioral Objectives* (Mimeographed). College Park, Maryland: Bureau of Educational Research, University of Maryland, 1966. Reproduced by permission, for which the authors express their thanks.

and shape of this object." The child's description is considered sufficiently complete when there is a probability that any other individual is able to use the description to identify the object or event.

7. *Stating a Rule.* Makes a verbal statement (not necessarily in technical terms) which conveys a rule or a principle, including the names of the proper classes of objects or events in their correct order. Example: "What is the test for determining whether this surface is flat?" The acceptable response requires the mention of the application of a straightedge, in various directions, to determine touching all along the edge for each position.

8. *Applying a Rule.* Using a learned principle or rule to derive an answer to a question. The answer may be correct identification, the supplying of a name, or some other kind of response. The question is stated in such a way that the individual must employ a rational process to arrive at the answer. Such a process may be simple, as "Property A is true, property B is true, therefore property C must be true."

9. *Demonstrating.* Performing the operations necessary to the application of a rule or principle. Example: "Show how you would tell whether this surface is flat." The answer requires that the individual use a straightedge to determine touching of the edge to the surface at all points, and in various directions.

10. *Interpreting.* The child should be able to identify objects and/or events in terms of their consequences. There will be a set of rules or principles always connected with this behavior.

The Result of the Behavior. The third component is the product, the performance, or the "what" the student is to do. Here are some examples of statements which include the first three components. The portion of the statement that appears in italics is the *result* of the behavior.

The student writes *a sentence.*
The learner walks *from point A to point B.*
The student spells aloud *the word "simple."*

To determine the result you can expect from students in an educational setting, you must first decide what you *want* them to do as a result of instruction and then write instructional objectives identifying *what* behavior is to be performed.

There are several ways to determine what to include in instructional objectives. Some educators have found it useful to examine old tests, since they are one indication of what students can do after instruction. Others have interviewed students who have mastered the desired behavior, determining *what* their terminal behavior for a course was and *how* they performed it. Still others have observed a student actually demonstrating mastery performance or have observed a product he produced (and the steps executed in producing it).

The Relevant Conditions Under Which the Behavior Is to Be Performed. What are the stimulus conditions to which the student will be expected to respond when demonstrating the desired behavior? To state this concern in less complex terms, "What are the *givens,* the *limitations,* the *restrictions* that are imposed on the student when he/she is demonstrating the terminal behavior?" Here are examples of some stimulus conditions that one might include in an instructional objective:

> "When presented with a typed list . . . "
> "Given a slide rule . . . "
> "Upon reading chapter 4 in *x* (insert name of textbook) . . . "
> "With the use of class notes . . . "
> "Without the use of class notes or other references . . . "

Now, let us turn to the question of how to determine the conditions under which the student will be expected to demonstrate mastery— conditions that are to be specified in the instructional objectives. Three suggestions are listed below:

1. Specify the information, tools, equipment, source materials, and anything else that will be available to the student to help him/her perform the terminal behavior required in the objective.
2. Specify the information, tools, equipment, source materials, and anything else that the student cannot use when demonstrating the terminal behavior.
3. List as many of the actual conditions as possible under which the student might be expected to demonstrate the terminal behavior in a real-life setting, and try to include as many of them in the objective as possible.

The Standard Which Will Be Used to Evaluate the Success of the Product or Performance. We noted earlier in this volume that instructional objectives provide information regarding *how effectively* a student must perform to demonstrate adequate mastery of a prescribed behavior. Readers also may recall that specifying the expected level of performance was one of the steps identified for formulating instructional objectives. In this section we discuss the relevant characteristics of standards required for determining the adequacy of responses.

Standard or *criterion* as used here refers to a basis for evaluating the prescribed behavior. Suppose you were told that you must throw a baseball fifty feet to perform the task successfully. The standard specified for determining whether you performed the task of throwing the baseball adequately is *fifty feet.*

A *performance standard*, then, is a specified level of achievement used to identify individuals who have mastered a task acceptably. *Achievement* here refers to performance in terms of its adequacy. We determine achievement by answering this question: "How effectively was a given task performed in respect to a specified criterion or standard?"

Several of the reasons for including performance standards in instructional objectives were mentioned previously. Performance standards help both teachers and students know where any given student is in any given program. They provide a minimal criterion and offer the potential of success to all students. Teachers find performance standards invaluable when preparing evaluative instruments and when determining the efficacy of their instructional programs. Mager (1962) indicates that when the minimum acceptable performance for each objective is specified, we have a performance standard to use in assessing instructional programs.

Classes of performance standards will now be considered. Various types of criteria may be used to determine mastery of given objectives. We will discuss some general types of performance standards as they relate to mastery level.

A specified level of mastery for objectives is generally determined arbitrarily, and it may have a wide range. In one case the teacher may want the student to be able to list "all five steps similarly to the way they are stated in the textbook." In another case, the teacher may determine that, "given a 100-word typed message and five minutes in which to do the task, a student will type the message on a separate piece of paper; a successful, finished product will include no more than two errors (typing or any other kind of error)." In the latter case, the teacher has required almost perfect performance (although some typing teachers known to the authors would not agree that this criterion approximates perfect performance).

Minimal mastery level refers to what a student has to do to "win the game"—to achieve an objective successfully. The typing objective described above asked for minimal mastery. For another example, consider the following phrase:

... to be able to identify *at least five* characteristics of . . .

Identification of five characteristics is the minimal mastery level acceptable in that example.

It is not possible to specify all the criteria for mastery level here because space is not available for a detailed discussion. However, here are some examples of different types of performance standards:

Minimum Number
"... must list *four* steps. . . ."
"... write all *ten words* presented accurately. . . ."
"... distinguish *three* main ideas. . . ."
Percent or Proportion
"... write (spell) accurately *100 percent* of the 10 words presented. . . ."
"... list *80 percent* of the verbs appearing in a 200-word message. . . ."
Limitation of Departure from Fixed Standard
"... must be correct to the *nearest percent*. . . ."
"... must be within *five decibels* of. . . ."
Distinguishing Features of Successful Performance
"... the radio plays within a *one-day period*. . . ."
"... all balls on the paper are *colored red*. . . ."

Examples of constraints are used above to specify performance standards in instructional objectives. They include limitations, restrictions, or confinements specifying or implying the conditions under which performance must occur to be successful. Consider the following example:

... to be able to walk a mile *within a ten-minute period.*

The constraint or restriction is *within a ten-minute period.* This phrase restricts the conditions (time limit) for successful terminal performance. One demonstrates mastery when one walks a mile "within a specified time period." Some examples of mastery level described above could be classified as constraints (e.g., "... three out of four words...."; "... 80 percent...."; "... must be correct to the nearest percent....").

A potential point of confusion regarding constraints is related to the fact that they deal with conditions under which the behavior is to be demonstrated. In one sense, then, it is reasonable to classify such constraints under stimulus conditions which influence how the behavior will be executed satisfactorily. However, while constraints do specify limiting conditions regarding how the task is to be executed, the emphasis in using constraints as performance standards *is on how satisfactorily*. Note that the time-limit example above told the learner those conditions within which he/she must operate to master the objective.

Accuracy of performance is another matter related to standards and one that borders on a semantic problem. Consider this example:

> Given 100 words presented orally by the teacher, the student will write down (spell) at least 80 percent of these words accurately. Accuracy will be determined by matching a student's responses on the written list to the correctly spelled words in the textbook (pp. x and y).

This objective has two standards worth distinguishing. The first standard, *"80 percent of these words,"* specifies the minimal level of mastery. The second standard states how the accuracy will be determined (i.e., how accurate responses can be defined operationally)—*"Accuracy will be ... the textbook (pp. x and y)."* Many writers of objectives specify the performance standard (how effective), but not *how* the accuracy of performance will be determined. We encourage you to include both of these types of standards in your instructional objectives.

Suggestions to the teacher are offered here, for specifying performance standards.

1. Select carefully the actual criteria (and levels) for ascertaining mastery. Should you select criteria based on behavior levels which discriminate between successful and unsuccessful performance? Should you specify criteria low enough for everyone to master them easily (which will make you look like a great instructor) or high enough so that only the most able can master the performance standard (which will probably make you look like a poor teacher)?

2. Use a variety of measures, and where possible, describe alternative means for evaluating objectives. For some objectives, various behaviors such as "to identify" or "to distinguish" could be required for the same or similar material to be mastered. Why not change the level of the performance standard according to the task?

A Program for Writing Instructional Objectives[2]

> The following pages contain
> the program text option (#2)
> described on page 33.

Program Objectives. The desired terminal behavior to be performed upon completion of this program follows: Given a content area in a subject area of your choosing, you will write at least two instructional objectives for the content area, using the five components of instructional objectives correctly. Two secondary objectives that also may be attained as you work through the program include the following:

1. Given five minutes, you will list and define, in writing, the five basic components of instructional objectives.
2. Given two instructional objectives, you will identify and label, in writing, the five basic components of instructional objectives for each objective given.

Instructions for Programed Materials. The instructional program that follows is designed to help you learn to write instructional objectives in a systematic, step-by-step manner. The information about objectives is presented a bit at a time. Each bit or frame, unless otherwise specified, requires you to write down one or more answers. *Please use a blank sheet of paper as an answer sheet* because sufficient space is not provided in the program to write most answers. After you write your response to the frame, you will receive immediate feedback regarding the correctness of

---

[2]Adapted from Donald J. Cegala, Robert J. Kibler, Larry L. Barker, and David T. Miles, "Writing Behavioral Objectives: A Programed Article," *The Speech Teacher* 21, 1972, 151–168. Reprinted by permission of the Speech Communication Association of America.

your answer. Accordingly, as you proceed through the program, the material on writing instructional objectives will be presented and, at the same time, you will receive feedback concerning appropriate answers about terms, principles, and concepts.

The frames begin at the top of each page and go down vertically to the bottom of the page. The first frame is followed by the second, third, and so on. Use a sheet of paper (different from your answer sheet) to cover (mask) the lower frames. Read each frame carefully, and then write your answer(s) on your sheet (another blank sheet of paper). After you have written your answer, slide the "masking paper" down the page, and you will receive feedback concerning your answer. Always go directly to the next successive frame, *unless you are instructed otherwise in the program.*

While going through this program, please try to remember that you are not taking a test but are learning about writing objectives. If, at times, it seems as though the material is repetitious, this is so because the program is constructed to reinforce principles or concepts learned earlier. Now, if you have your two sheets of blank paper, you are ready to begin.

1

Instructional objectives are composed of five basic components. The first of these components, and easiest to remember, is *who is to perform the desired behavior.*

2

Obviously, the student is to demonstrate the behavior. When writing instructional objectives, other terms such as "learner," "pupil," and "enrollee" may be used instead of the term "student." The label used is not important. What is important is that you specify _____.

3

You should have written: *who is to perform the desired behavior.* This is the first component of the five components in instructional objectives.

4

The second component of instructional objectives is *the specific observable act (or behavior) that the learner is to perform.* For example, if you desire the learner to draw a right triangle, then you should indicate the specific behavior the learner is to perform, i.e., "to diagram" or "to draw." The key point to remember is that the behavior specified must be an observable act, i.e., "to write," "to speak," "to list," etc.

5

The second component of instructional objectives is_____
_____. It is important to remember that the behavior specified must be_____.

6

You should have written: *the specific observable act (or behavior) that the learner is to perform* and *an observable act.*

To help you keep these points in mind, you should begin to use "action verbs"[3] to indicate clearly what class of behavior is to be performed by the learner. Some examples of "action verbs" are:

1. identify   6. describe
2. distinguish   7. evaluate
3. construct   8. apply
4. name   9. locate
5. order   10. interpret

Compare these two objectives:

1. The student will know the five steps of reflective thinking.
2. The student will list in writing the five steps of reflective thinking.

---

[3]Much confusion exists here since action verbs are not always behavioral verbs. See Roger E. Robinson and David T. Miles, "Behavioral Objectives: An Even Closer Look," *Educational Technology,* 1971, 39–44, for a discussion of this topic. Also, for a listing of action verbs, see H. M. Harmes, *Behavioral Analysis of Learning Objectives* (West Palm Beach, Florida: Harmes and Associates, 1969).

Which objective most clearly specifies the desired behavior?

_____

7

The correct response is objective 2: "The student will list in writing the five steps of reflective thinking."

Although we may have a reasonable degree of common meaning for the term "know," the question still remains: what do we mean when we say the learner should *know* the five steps of reflective thinking? Do we want the learner to apply the five steps, recite them, criticize them? It really is not clear. However, the phrase "list in writing," as it is used in objective 2 in Frame 6, indicates exactly what the learner is to *do* when demonstrating that he "knows" or "understands" the five steps of reflective thinking.

Which of the following objectives meets the criteria we have discussed thus far?

1. The student will understand the main points in a story.
2. The student will write a five-sentence paragraph.
3. Draw a rectangle.
4. The student will know Ohm's law.
5. The student will orally apply principles of effective dramatic reading.

8

You should have selected objectives 2 and 5. If you were correct, go to Frame 10; if not, go on to frame 9 (below).

9

Recall that the two components of instructional objectives discussed thus far are:

1. Who is to perform the desired behavior;
2. The specific observable act (or behavior) that the learner is to perform.

The first component now should be easy to remember. The student (pupil, learner, etc.) is the one who is to perform the behavior. Objective 3 in Frame 7 is incorrect because the first component of instructional objectives is missing: *who* is to perform the behavior. Written correctly, the objective should read: "The student will draw a rectangle."

In order to keep the second component in mind, you should become familiar with the "action verbs" listed in Frame 6. These "action verbs" clearly indicate what class of behavior the learner (student, pupil, etc.) is to perform. Therefore, objectives 1 and 4 in Frame 7 are incorrect because "know" and "understand" are not clear indicators of the *observable* behavior which the student is to perform. The terms "list," "define," or "apply" would have been much clearer because they indicate what observable behavior the student is to perform.

-Go to Frame 12-

10

Good show!! You were able to identify the correct objectives. You are almost ready to begin writing your own objectives. However, before moving to the third component of instructional objectives, indicate below the first two components of instructional objectives, and list as many "action verbs" as you can.

1. _____

2. _____

1. _____   6. _____
2. _____   7. _____
3. _____   8. _____
4. _____   9. _____
5. _____   10. _____

11

The correct responses are:

1. Who is to perform the desired behavior.
2. The specific observable act (or behavior) that the learner is to perform.

1. identify	6. describe
2. distinguish	7. evaluate
3. construct	8. apply
4. name	9. locate
5. order	10. interpret

12

The third component of instructional objectives is *the product, performance, or result of the student's behavior.* The product, performance, or result of the student's behavior may be "a speech," "an essay," "a successful dyadic interchange," etc. Some examples of objectives containing this component and the other two components discussed previously are listed below. The third component is underlined in the objectives.

1. The student will identify in writing three causes of the Civil War.
2. The student will orally participate in a policy-making discussion using Dewey's five steps of reflective thinking.
3. The student will write a definition of democracy.

13

Before you attempt to write an instructional objective using the three components we have discussed thus far, let's be sure you remember what these components are.

By now you probably remember that the first two components are:

1. Who is to perform the behavior.

2. What is the specific observable act (or behavior) to be performed.
What is the third component?

3. _____

` ------------------------------   ---

14

You are correct if you said *the product (or performance or result) of
the student's behavior.* If your response was incorrect, perhaps you should
turn back to Frame 12 and re-read the material before going on.

15

You are now ready to write an objective using the three components
we have discussed thus far. Below is a list of six terms. Select three of the
terms or phrases and order them to form an instructional objective.

   1. know   3. define in writing   5. the student will
   2. the teacher will   4. four steps in analyz-   6. understand
                              ing a proposition

16

The correct response is 5, 3, 4.

*The student will define in writing four steps in analyzing a
proposition.*

If you did not select 5, 3, 4, go to Frame 17; if you did select 5, 3, 4, go to
Frame 18.

17

It seems you are having a few problems!

One set of alternatives you should have chosen between is "the teacher will" and "the student will." Although objectives sometimes are prepared for teachers, they most often are prepared for students. Therefore, the first component of your objective (who is to perform the behavior) should have been "the student."

You should have chosen one term among "know," "understand," and "define in writing." Recall that the terms "know" and "understand" really do not clearly indicate what the student is to *do* in demonstrating his/her knowledge or understanding. The term "define in writing," however, specifically indicates to the student what he/she is to *do* in demonstrating competence. Therefore, "define in writing" is the correct response.

Recall the third component of instructional objectives is the product, performance, or result of the student's behavior. In this instance, the product to be produced is "the four steps in analyzing a proposition."

-Go to Frame 18-

18

By now you know that the second and third components of instructional objectives indicate what behavior the student is to perform and the end product or result of his/her performance. Although these components provide more clarity to students than most nonbehavioral objectives, it is often necessary to define further the behavior you are after by specifying *conditions you will impose upon the student when he/she is demonstrating the behavior.* In other words, what are the "conditions," the "limitations," the "restrictions" that are imposed on the student when he/she is performing the stated behavior? Some examples of these conditions are:

1. Given one hour and a list of ten historical events . . .
2. Without use of the textbook or notes the student will . . .
3. After hearing a 30-minute tape-recorded speech, the student will . . .
4. Without referring to his/her outline, the student will . . .

19

Below are three suggestions for determining the conditions under which the student will be expected to demonstrate the required behavior:

1. Specify the information, equipment, source materials, and anything else that will be available to the student when performing the required behavior.
2. Specify the information, equipment, source materials and anything else that will *not* be available to the student when performing the required behavior.
3. List as many as possible of the actual conditions under which the student might be expected to demonstrate the terminal behavior in a real-life setting, and try to include as many of them in the objective as possible.

20

Given the preceding discussion, you should now be aware that the fourth component of instructional objectives is *the relevant conditions under which the behavior is to be performed.*

Let's see how successful we were in explaining this component. Which part of the objective below tells the student something about the conditions under which the behavior is to be performed?

1. Given a five-minute tape-recorded story and 20 minutes,
2. the student will write a paragraph retelling the events of the story.

If you selected:
    #1—go to Frame 22.
    #2—go to Frame 21.

21

Ooops! You selected the portion of the objective that reads: *the student will write a paragraph retelling the events of the story.*

You are probably still thinking of the second and third components of instructional objectives, the behavior to be performed and the product to be produced. Try not to get these components confused with *the relevant conditions under which the behavior is to be performed.* Perhaps you should turn back to Frame 18 and re-read the material concerning the fourth component of instructional objectives.

When you have done that, go to Frame 23.

22

Congratulations! You selected the correct response—*"Given a five-minute tape-recorded story and 20 minutes..."* The portion of the objective you selected indicated to the student that he/she would be given a story, the relative length of the story, the mode of communication it would be in, and the maximum time the learner would have to perform the required behavior.

23

Does the objective below contain the fourth component of instructional objectives?

Given a test, the student will demonstrate effective application of the rules of punctuation.

24

The answer is both yes and no.

The objective does provide the student with some information about the condition under which he/she is to perform the behavior, i.e., "given a test."

However, some relevant conditions are not indicated to the student. For example, will the test be oral or written? Will the test be essay or multiple-choice? How long will the test be? How much time will the student have to complete the test?

We might then rephrase the objective to read:

> Given 20 written unpunctuated sentences and one hour, the student will rewrite and correctly punctuate at least 16 sentences.

25

Look at the objective in Frame 24 (above) again. Did you notice anything different about this objective from other examples of objectives given thus far?

Another component has been added to the objective. Can you identify the component?

26

The fifth component added to the objective in Frame 24 is the *standard (or criterion) which will be used to evaluate the success of the product or performance.*

> The criterion in the example is: correctly punctuate at least 16 sentences.

Look at the complete objective again:

> Given 20 written unpunctuated sentences and one hour, the student will rewrite and correctly punctuate at least 16 sentences.

This component often is the most difficult to understand and use correctly. Let's examine the component more closely.

27

The *standard* or *criterion* refers to the basis for evaluating the prescribed behavior. Suppose you were asked to perform the following behavior:

Run the 50-yard dash.

As stated, you might infer that your performance would be evaluated on the basis of whether or not you were able to run fifty yards without stopping for a breather! But suppose we assumed that you were healthy and we desired to impose a time limit on your performance. The behavior might then be stated:

Run the 50-yard dash within 8 seconds.

It is now clear that your running performance will be evaluated on the basis of the eight-second standard or criterion. This standard is the *minimum acceptable performance* for achieving the objective successfully.

28

Several types of criteria may be used to determine the minimum level of acceptable performance for objectives. Some examples of different types of performance standards appear below:

1. ... must list *four* steps ...
2. ... distinguish *at least three* main ideas ...
3. ... identify *80 percent* of the forms of support ...
4. ... must be correct to the *nearest percent* ...
5. ... must list *all* of the principles ...
6. ... must match in meaning *with the textbook* ...
7. ... must satisfy *80 percent* of the student's personal criteria ...
8. ... communicate an idea to *90 percent* of the students ...

29

Does the objective stated below contain a standard?

Given a list of 20 incomplete sentences requiring adjectives, the student will write the adjectives to complete the sentences within 15 minutes.

30

If you answered "yes," you are probably confusing the fourth and fifth components of instructional objectives. Recall that the fourth component specifies the *relevant conditions* under which the behavior is to be demonstrated. True, such conditions do influence the manner in which the behavior will be executed satisfactorily, but they do not indicate *how satisfactorily* the behavior is to be performed.
Read the following objective:

Given a list of 20 incomplete sentences requiring adjectives, the student will write adjectives to complete the sentences within 15 minutes.

The relevant conditions under which the behavior is to be performed are specified (i.e., given a list of twenty sentences requiring adjectives and a fifteen-minute time limit), but the standard or criterion to be used in *evaluating* performance is not included. For example, the objective does not state how many sentences must be written correctly or what standard will be used to judge correctness.

31

Which objective below contains the standard or criterion component?

1. Given 30 minutes, the student will list in writing the types of government other than democracy and compare each type with democracy.

2. Given 30 minutes, the student will write an essay comparing and contrasting the democratic form of government with three other types of government. The product must contain at least one point of comparison and one point of contrast for each of the three types of government.

If you selected:

#1—go to Frame 33.
#2—go to Frame 32.

32

Good! You're getting the hang of it now. You recognized that the portion of the objective which stated: "... at least one point of comparison and one point of contrast for each of the three types of government" specified the standard or criterion for evaluation of student performance.

-Go to Frame 34-

33

Ooops! Look more carefully at the first objective. Note that the objective does not indicate how many types of government other than democracy the student must list. In other words, the minimum acceptable performance is not specified. Compare the first objective to the second one listed. The second objective indicates that *three types* of governments must be discussed. Note the last part of the second objective, "... the product must contain at least one point of comparison and one point of contrast for each of the three types of government." This part of the objective indicates the minimum standard of performance which the student must demonstrate.

Got it? Let's see ...

-Go to Frame 34-

34

Which objective below contains the standard or criterion component?

1. Given one hour in class, the student will identify and describe in writing the role and function of freedom of speech in a democracy.
2. Given a list of 10 famous scientists, the student will identify and describe in writing at least 8 of the 10 scientists' major contributions to knowledge.

If you selected:

#1—go to Frame 35.
#2—go to Frame 36.

35

You missed again! You selected: "Given one hour, the student will identify and describe in writing the role and function of freedom of speech in a democracy." Where is the standard in this objective?

Perhaps you should return to Frame 26 and re-read the material concerning the fifth component of instructional objectives. Then go to Frame 37.

36

Now you are getting it! " . . . at least 8 of the 10 scientists . . . " indicates an 80 percent criterion for performance.

—Go to Frame 37—

37

One more point is worth noting concerning the criterion component of instructional objectives. Consider the following objective:

Given a 30-minute essay quiz, the student will identify and describe in writing at least three of the similarities and differences between classical conditioning and instrumental conditioning. The essay will be evaluated on the extent to which it reflects points covered in assigned readings and class discussion concerning the two methods of conditioning.

The objective has two standards worth distinguishing. The first standard, "at least three," specifies the *minimum level* of acceptable performance. The second standard " . . . evaluated on the extent to which it reflects points covered in assigned readings and class discussion . . . ," states *how* accuracy will be determined. Many writers of instructional objectives specify the minimum level of acceptable performance, but not how the accuracy of the performance will be determined. You are encouraged to include both standards in writing instructional objectives.

Frame 38 provides some examples of objectives with both standards included.

38

1. Given 30 minutes, the student will draw a diagram indicating *at least five* major components of a plant cell and describe the relationships among the components *as presented in the textbook.*
2. Given one hour, the student will identify and describe in writing *at least five* methods for organizing messages *as they are presented in the textbook.*
3. Given 30 minutes, the student will describe in writing the scientific method and list *at least four* ways it differs from other methods of inquiry. *The product will be evaluated by the extent to which responses reflect information contained in assigned readings and class discussion.*

39

Now you should be able to identify all five components of instructional objectives. Here is an instructional objective. Underline (or write out

on a separate piece of paper) each of the five components and label each
component.

Given ten mixed numbers and proper fractions, the student
will show in writing all the steps necessary to divide at least
eight correctly.

40

If this program has been successful, your response should look like
this:

4   1

Given ten mixed numbers and proper fractions, | | the student

2   3

| | will show in writing | | all the steps necessary to divide | | at

5

least eight correctly.

1. Who is to perform the behavior.
2. The observable act (or behavior) to be performed.
3. The product, performance, or result of the behavior.
4. The relevant conditions under which the behavior is to be performed.
5. The standard (or criterion) used to evaluate the behavior.

41

Since it is important for you to be able to identify all 5 components of
instructional objectives before you begin writing your own objectives, try
to identify the components in this objective:

Given five typewritten argumentative paragraphs and one
hour, the student will identify in writing: (1) evidence,
(2) warrant, (3) claim, (4) reservation, and (5) support for the
warrant for each argument. Performance will be evaluated by
the extent to which the student identifies correctly four of the
five items listed above for each argumentative paragraph.

42

The five components are:

                4

Given five typewritten argumentative paragraphs and one

        1   2

hour,| | the student| | will identify in writing:| | (1) evidence,

  3

(2) warrant, (3) claim, (4) reservations, and (5) support for the

                          5

warrant for each argument.| | Performance will be evaluated by

the extent to which the student identifies correctly four of the

five items listed above for each argumentative paragraph.

1. Who is to perform the behavior.
2. The observable act (or behavior) to be performed.
3. The product, performance, or result of the behavior.
4. The relevant conditions under which the behavior is to be performed.
5. The standard (or criterion) used to evaluate the behavior.

43

Now try to write an instructional objective. Suppose you were teaching students to conjugate irregular Spanish verbs. In addition, you are interested in students being able to translate the Spanish conjugates into English. Write an instructional objective expressing these ideas to your students.

_____

_____

_____

_____

_____

_____

44

The exact wording may vary, but you should have written something like this:

> Given a list of 20 Spanish irregular verbs and one hour, the student will conjugate at least 18 verbs correctly (i.e., as shown in the textbook) and translate them to their correct English equivalents.

Well, how did you do?

Try writing an instructional objective for this situation:

Suppose you wanted students to apply some principles of effective adaptive listening that you had been discussing for a few days in class. To make life easier, let's say you had access to a ten-minute taped recording of an informative speech which had been recorded with interfering noise. In addition, you have a twenty-five-item multiple-choice test over material in the speech. "Put it all together," and write an objective for students including the relevant conditions stated above.

_____

_____

_____

_____

_____

45

Again, wording may vary, but essentially you should have written:

> Given a 10-minute tape-recorded informative speech and simultaneous presentation of interfering noise (e.g., white noise, music, conversation, etc.), the student will demonstrate application of principles of effective adaptive listening. Acceptable performance will be a score of 70 percent or better on a 25-item, multiple-choice comprehension test over material contained in the speech.

46

If you have never written an instructional objective before, our guess is that you probably didn't do extremely well! Perhaps a little more practice is needed. Try writing an objective for this situation:

You have a unit on voice control in an oral interpretation class. The class will be taught how to apply specific criteria in evaluating proper voice control. You usually play a five-minute tape-recorded oral reading to your class and ask them to write a critique of the speaker's use of voice control to determine if the students can apply the evaluative criteria you have taught them. How would you specify this instructional intent in an instructional objective format?

47

Your objective should look something like this:

Given a 5-minute tape-recorded oral reading and 20 minutes, the student will write a critique of the speaker's use of voice control in presenting the selection. The product will be evaluated by the extent to which the student employs the evaluative criteria presented in assigned readings and class lectures.

Getting better? Try writing an objective for the situation described in the next frame.

48

Try your hand at writing an objective for this situation.

You are teaching a course in acting and have a unit on improvisation. In the past you have required students to improvise assigned roles in specific situations. You would like to continue this practice because the students enjoy the assignment. Your main concern in the unit is that students are convincing (i.e., believable) in the roles that they improvise.

49

Your instructional objective should look something like this:

Given a written statement describing a situation involving two of the following person-roles—a parent, student, teacher, administrator, spouse—the student will improvise an assigned person-role for six minutes with a classmate. Performance will be evaluated by the extent to which the class agrees that the improvisation was believable as indicated by responses on a rating form.

How did you do on that one? If you are experiencing problems, don't worry. Writing good instructional objectives is not easy; it requires time, effort, and *practice*. Hopefully, you now have the skills which will allow you to practice writing instructional objectives. Go to it! Happy writing and teaching!!

THE BEGINNING . . .

DIFFICULTIES ENCOUNTERED IN SPECIFYING INSTRUCTIONAL OBJECTIVES

Problems will be encountered as you specify instructional objectives. We have identified a few of these difficulties so you may watch for them as you formulate this type of objective. Some of the problems identified here were first encountered in a thoughtful report prepared by Ammerman and Melching (1966).

Sometimes an instructor fails to specify important performance standards because the information is not readily available for an instructional decision. Be careful not to be satisfied with less important objectives just because measuring devices are available or because certain behaviors are easy to measure. If a complex learning operation is important but not included in an objective, break it down into its component parts and develop standards to assess the level of mastery of each part. If we do not have standards for successful performance, we should begin developing them, and now is as good a time as any.

Another potential difficulty is associated with utility. What is the mastery for? While it may be convenient to measure whether three out of four steps of x process are included in a written statement, maybe all four steps must be demonstrated actually to use the process; mastery of three steps may be of little or no value. Moreover, the value of mastery becomes even more clear when the total process of learning is considered. Today's instructional objectives are used to create tomorrow's preinstructional evaluation for the next higher level of instruction.

A problem somewhat related to utility is making the objectives relevant to the task (i.e., derived from the known work requirements for a given job or learning task). Those activities in which students are required to engage that are not required in a work situation or in a higher order learning level may be of limited value. There is also the possibility of stating instructional objectives (and particularly performance standards) that are related primarily to a testing situation rather than to the next set or ultimate learning operation to be acquired.

Still another problem is related to the teacher's knowing what objectives he/she wants to achieve and communicating his/her knowledge to the student. If the instructor has not specified instructional objectives, one could infer that he/she has not decided what students should be able to do as a result of instruction. Missing performance standards or other incomplete information in instructional objectives invites similar inferences from outside observers, like colleagues, parents, and administrators.

A difficult but important task for the teacher is to arrange instructional objectives and performance standards for given instructional objectives into a priority list. It is critical to learning to arrange the priorities for given tasks into an efficient order to increase learning. It is just as important to arrange the priority of performance standards (and to use several of them) to determine the mastery required for a given objective. Regarding students' mastery of objectives, it also is important for the teacher to remember that the potential measurement error in evaluation procedures should be considered. Errors in measurement may account for a student's meeting the criterion "accidentally" or failing to meet it when he/she should have.

SUMMARY

This chapter focused on the first component of the general model of instruction—instructional objectives. Instructional objectives were distinguished from other types of educational objectives in terms of specificity and purpose. Three options were then offered for learning how to write instructional objectives. The first option described and illustrated each component of instructional objectives in a textbook format. The second option consisted of a programed text that described and illustrated components of instructional objectives and, in addition, provided opportunity for practice in writing instructional objectives. The third option, which provides for maximum learning, consisted of both the first and second options. The chapter concluded with a discussion of selected difficulties encountered in specifying instructional objectives and offered suggestions to reduce those difficulties.

3

PREASSESSMENT

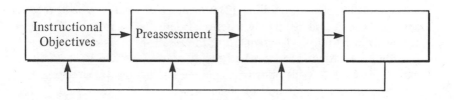

After completing this chapter, the learner should be able to:

1. State three reasons why preassessment of learners is conducted prior to beginning instruction;
2. State three types of information that the results of preassessment provide;
3. Describe the purpose of a preassessment test of entry behavior;
4. State why standardized tests often are inappropriate preassessment measures;
5. Describe a strategy for developing a preassessment test of entry behavior;
6. Distinguish between preassessment of entry behavior and preassessment of terminal behavior;
7. Describe a strategy for developing a preassessment test of terminal behavior;
8. State the ultimate goal of preassessment.

This chapter is concerned with preassessment, the second component of the general model of instruction. In essence, preassessment involves evaluation of student performance, but the purposes for which evaluation is intended in preassessment are different from the typical purposes for which evaluation procedures are used. Teachers most often use evaluation procedures for assessing students' performance at the end of a unit of instruction. Bloom, Hastings, and Madaus (1971) have referred to this type of assessment as summative evaluation. In our model, summative evaluation procedures would be used, for example, to assess students' mastery of instructional objectives after completing a unit of instruction. However, as the term implies, preassessment procedures are not used to assess students' performance after instruction but, rather, to assess their performance *before* instruction begins.

Preassessment of learners prior to beginning instruction is designed to determine: (1) whether learners have the prerequisite behavioral capabilities for the instruction to follow, (2) how much of what is to be learned is already known, and (3) the instructional activities that should be presented to each student. Consequently, the results of preassessment should provide information (1) as to whether any students should be required to master prerequisite skills prior to beginning instruction, (2) as to whether any students may *omit* any of the instructional objectives, and (3) for prescribing specific instructional activities for specific students.

PREASSESSMENT OF ENTRY BEHAVIOR

Learner behaviors related to prerequisite capabilities for instruction often are called entry behaviors. As the term implies, entry behaviors are the behavioral capabilities resulting from previous learning that the student brings with him/her to the new instructional event. DeCecco (1968) points out that a preassessment test of entry behaviors is *not* designed to evaluate learners' ability to demonstrate terminal performance before instruction begins; rather, it is designed to evaluate relevant (i.e., to instructional objectives) learner capabilities resulting from previous learning. As such, the preassessment test of entry behaviors *ideally* should be related to instructional objectives, but only insofar as the test assesses prior learning relevant to capabilities needed to master new instructional objectives.

Teachers often are tempted to use various standardized tests of intelligence, achievement, and aptitude to assess students' entry behavior. However, these tests often are inappropriate preassessment measures, since in most instances the results cannot be used to describe students' entry behavior related to particular instructional objectives. The teacher may

find some standardized personality tests and attitude tests useful in preassessing students' entry behavior regarding some affective goals; but again,
these tests often do not directly relate to specific instructional objectives.
Consequently, the teacher typically is required to develop a preassessment
test designed to evaluate learners' entry behavior.

Development of a preassessment test for sequentially dependent units
of instruction (i.e., where mastery of each unit or course is necessary for
succeeding in subsequent units or courses) can be facilitated by examining
the instructional objectives employed in the preceding course(s). When
previously used instructional objectives are not available or when preassessment is desired for sequentially independent units of instruction, test
development may be facilitated by continuously asking and answering the
question: What entering capabilities must the learner demonstrate to
benefit maximally from the instruction to follow?

While the answer(s) to this question may on the surface appear
difficult to obtain, the complexity is minimized for at least two reasons.
First, teachers generally are quite sensitive to the basic prerequisite capabilities needed for students to master given units of instruction, particularly those units taught at the beginning of a course. Second, instructional
objectives provide even further guidance for the teacher in determining
what prerequisite capabilities are needed to master given instructional
units. For example, a teacher of an intermediate level course in Spanish
probably is quite sensitive to the basic capabilities that students should
have acquired in a fundamental course. Moreover, by examining instructional objectives for the intermediate course (particularly those pertaining
to the beginning unit[s]), the teacher should not experience extreme
difficulty in answering the question: What entering capabilities must the
learner demonstrate to benefit maximally from the instruction to follow?
Answers to the question may result, for example, in a preassessment test
designed to evaluate students' knowledge of key vocabulary words, irregular verb conjugates, and basic syntax rules. The results of the test may
indicate that some or all students require additional instruction to master
prerequisite skills prior to beginning instruction on the intermediate level.

PREASSESSMENT OF TERMINAL BEHAVIOR

The second reason for preassessment prior to beginning instruction is
to determine how much of what is to be learned is already known. This

type of preassessment is designed to determine whether any students may omit any instructional objectives. The distinction between preassessment of entry behavior and preassessment of terminal behavior is that the latter measures terminal performance (i.e., as stated in course or unit instructional objectives) prior to instruction. The clever reader will note that both types of preassessment can be accomplished simultaneously by using a test designed to assess entry behavior and terminal behavior (e.g., a portion of the test for entry and a portion for terminal). However, if for some reason the teacher must choose between the two, we recommend that preassessment focus on terminal behavior. Our recommendation is based on the assumption that in many instances most students will have at least minimal prerequisite capabilities. Even so, a word of caution is in order. If preassessment focuses only on terminal behavior, the teacher should avoid interpreting results as indicative of entry behavior capabilities. For example, a score of zero on a preassessment test of terminal behavior does not necessarily indicate that students lack prerequisite capabilities; it indicates only that they do not already know what is to be learned. Desired information about students' entry behavior can be provided only by procedures (e.g., test items) designed to assess prerequisite capabilities.

Ideally, preassessment test items of terminal behavior should be arranged hierarchically, if possible. This procedure is particularly useful if preassessment is to be done on a unit-by-unit basis. For example, Figure 3 depicts a learning hierarchy for a unit on ordering numbers. (In chapter 6 we will discuss learning hierarchies more completely.) One or more instructional objectives and corresponding test items may be specified for each stage of the hierarchy. The preassessment test of terminal behavior ideally would consist of test items designed to evaluate students' mastery of instructional objectives at each stage of the hierarchy. The results of this preassessment would provide the teacher with specific information about where each student is in the hierarchy and, consequently, which students may omit specific instructional objectives.

Of course, not all subject matters are amenable to hierarchical arrangement. Some subject areas are best suited to a flat structure, vertical structure, or mixed structure (see Briggs, 1968). Even so, the same basic procedure can be used for preassessment testing—e.g., assessing students' mastery of terminal behavior across the instructional objectives for a given

---

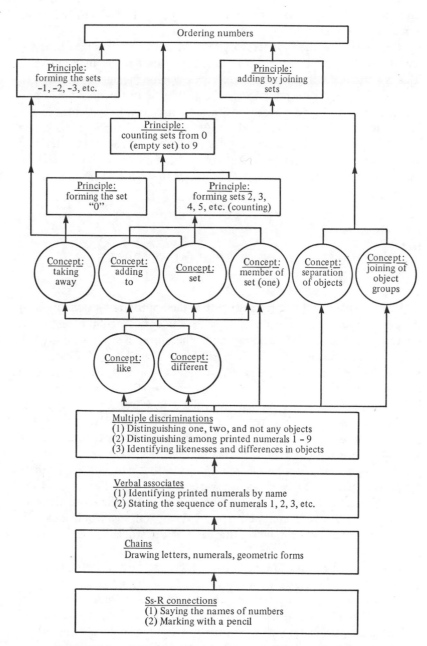

FIGURE 3. A Learning Hierarchy for Ordering Numbers

unit and using the results to determine how much of what is to be learned students already know.

Sometimes teachers prefer to preassess students' terminal behavior across instructional objectives for an entire course rather than one unit. This is particularly appropriate for courses where students are allowed to "test out" of a course prior to the beginning of instruction. When pre-assessment of this nature is desired, the test may consist of items that are representative of instructional objectives within each unit of the entire course. In this case the teacher may use preassessment results to determine which students may omit given units of instruction or be allowed to take more extensive (i.e., complete) terminal posttests for given units of instruction.

PRESCRIBING SPECIFIC INSTRUCTIONAL ACTIVITIES

The ultimate goal of preassessment is the appropriate prescription of specific instructional activities for each student. When the teacher is limited by time and/or facilities and, therefore, is unable to specify individual instructional activities for students, some form of subgrouping with different levels of objectives for different groups is the only feasible solution. This solution is of course most undesirable for sequential subjects, such as reading and mathematics, since many students are typically "passed" to the next course or grade without having achieved the level of performance considered necessary for succeeding in the next course. These students eventually build up a cumulative deficiency that makes academic success impossible. In subjects and courses that are not sequentially dependent, it is probably unnecessary to attempt to get all students to master the same level of achievement. When this is the case, different performance standards may be specified for different individuals or groups, and this can be done on the basis of the student's preassessment performance.

Hopefully the trend toward individualized, self-paced instruction will continue and will eventually reduce or eliminate the problems inherent in instruction that is group-paced and controlled by fixed time schedules for completing units and courses. Additional strategies available to the teacher for instructing several groups of students at various levels of achievement include performance contracting and peer-group instruction.

ADDITIONAL COMMENTS ABOUT PREASSESSMENT

Preassessment is probably most essential when an instructor is beginning a unit of instruction and he/she is unfamiliar with students' skills, knowledge, and attitudes regarding the material to be covered in the unit. However, in situations where instructors have the same students for a semester or a year, preassessment for each unit may be unnecessary. In courses that are sequential in nature, the successful completion of one unit should serve as evidence of the student's capability of entering the next unit. Thus an extensive preassessment would only be necessary at the beginning of a course sequence or semester-long course.

For shorter units (e.g., one week to a month) not in a sequential progression, less extensive preassessment would be appropriate. A few items from the end-of-unit evaluation could be used. A short interview with each student or an informal class discussion could be employed to reveal the general level of students' preparation for beginning the unit. By such informal techniques students who appear to have either considerable knowledge or inadequate knowledge regarding the objectives to be achieved for a unit can be identified and provided with a more extensive preassessment to determine what specific objectives can be omitted and what specific prerequisite skills are needed.

An extensive discussion of the various methods of preassessment is beyond the scope of this book. However, it is important for the teacher to employ some method of preassessing students' entry behavior and terminal behavior to determine the most appropriate instructional procedures for achieving instructional objectives. Teachers may find the appropriate assistance in developing valid preassessment methods by examining one of the several valuable sources on test construction and evaluation.

SUMMARY

Three purposes of preassessment were discussed in this chapter: preassessment of entry behavior, preassessment of terminal behavior, and preassessment for prescribing specific instructional activities. Procedures were discussed briefly for implementing preassessment for all three purposes.

4

INSTRUCTIONAL PROCEDURES[1]

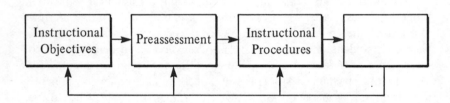

After completing this chapter, the learner should be able to:

1. State four steps involved in the design of instructional procedures;
2. Describe how each of the following is related to the design of instructional procedures:

(a) prelearning procedures   (f) practice
(b) learner motivation   (g) knowledge of results
(c) models of terminal performance   (h) graduated sequence
(d) active responding   (i) individual differences
(e) guidance   (j) classroom teaching performance

3. List ten commonly used modes of instruction and describe how each is related to the ten principles of instructional design;

[1]Major portions of this chapter were adapted from David T. Miles and Roger E. Robinson, "The General Teaching Model" (Unpublished manuscript). Educational Research Bureau, Southern Illinois University, 1969. Reprinted by permission of the authors.

4. Describe at least two ways in which research on attitudes can be applied to instruction designed to achieve goals in the affective domain;
5. List and describe five generalizations about the design of instructional procedures for achieving goals in the affective domain.

After students have been preassessed and adjustments made, such as adding or eliminating objectives or requiring prerequisite learning, the instructional procedures are implemented. The design of the instructional procedures involves (1) choosing the mode(s) of instruction that appear most efficient for getting most students to achieve the specified objectives; (2) selecting available instructional materials (e.g., books, films, lesson plans); (3) preparing new instructional materials when necessary; and (4) developing a sequential plan that takes students from where they are at the beginning of a unit to mastery of the unit objectives.

SELECTED PRINCIPLES FOR DESIGNING INSTRUCTIONAL PROCEDURES

When possible, decisions about instructional procedures should be based upon research evidence. The ten generalizations specified below are, to a large extent, based upon research evidence and are examples of principles that should be consulted in designing instructional activities. It should be noted that every application of these principles will not automatically apply to all students and all subject matters. Students vary in the way they learn, subject matters vary in their structures, and teachers vary in the way they interpret and apply principles of instruction. Thus application of these principles in each situation and with each student must be continually tested. The ten principles are discussed below.

1. Prelearning Preparation. Learners must have mastered prerequisite behaviors in order to succeed in those behaviors they are required to learn. Learners also should be prepared for new learning experiences by warming up, being informed of what previously learned behaviors will be helpful or harmful, and acquiring an appropriate "set" (predisposition to respond in a particular way) for what is to follow. For example, a preview at the beginning of a chapter or film can increase learning efficiency. Providing students with the instructional objectives for a unit also has been found to facilitate learning.

TABLE 1. *Motivation for Learning*

Goal or Incentive	"The student learns (to add fractions, or write paragraphs, or build models) because . . ."	How Motivation May be Developed and Maintained
1. To know.	. . . he/she just likes to know the how and why of things. Satisfying his/her curiosity or acquiring knowledge and skill is what it's all about—whether he/she ever uses what is learned is unimportant (epistemic curiosity).	Provide opportunities for the student to inquire and learn about whatever turns him/her on. Supply information and materials only when requested. Give no extrinsic rewards (praise, grades, etc.) for learning.
2. To be able to do something related to what is learned in the distant future. (Delayed intrinsic)	. . . he/she will eventually be able to use what is learned to do pleasureful and necessary things—i.e., read good novels, complete income tax forms, understand scientific advances, vote intelligently, raise children.	Show and frequently remind the student of the eventual value of what he/she is to learn. Encourage self-directed learning, minimize teacher-directed learning, and use no extrinsic rewards.
3. To be able to do something related to what is learned at the present time. (Immediate intrinsic)	. . . he/she needs the knowledge or skill to do something desirable now—i.e., play a game, write a poem, identify trees, communicate ideas, fix a car, train an animal, understand Apollo 11.	Provide or arrange opportunities for the student to do things which require learning. Expose potentially interesting things; pose tasks, games, questions, problems; suggest projects; supply information, materials, encouragement, and feedback; provide frequent opportunities to use what is learned.

74

Goal or Incentive	"The student learns (to add fractions, or write paragraphs, or build models) because . . ."	How Motivation May be Developed and Maintained
4. To obtain future benefits and rewards unrelated to what is learned. (Delayed extrinsic)	. . . he/she wants to pass tests, get good grades, obtain a degree, receive awards and honors, get a good job, own three cars and an Irish wolfhound; he/she may also want to gain the respect and admiration of parents, friends, or professional community.	Use minimal extrinsic rewards. Point out and remind the student of potential future rewards for present efforts. Use some immediate extrinsic rewards when future reward is distant, but reduce their use as student progresses.
5. To obtain immediate benefits and rewards unrelated to what is learned. (Immediate extrinsic)	. . . he/she wants to obtain immediate rewards such as the following: a) social rewards—smiles, verbal praise from teacher, parents, peers; b) general rewards—free time, choice of activities, money; c) specific rewards—gold star, food, toys, field trip, play ball.	Identify or develop effective rewards (reinforcers, i.e., things the student wants), systematically deliver rewards for appropriate behavior, and withhold for inappropriate behavior. Use tokens or point system to facilitate observation.

2. Motivation. Students are more efficient if they have a desire to learn what is being taught. This desire can be promoted by convincing learners of the value of mastering the subject matter and by making goals that they already desire (e.g., acquisition of desired information or skills, social approval, grades, etc.) available to them for accomplishing learning objectives. Selecting subject matter that interests and/or permits students to participate in planning their educational activities can increase their desire to learn. The learning task should be presented in such a way that the learner feels challenged and also confident that he/she can succeed. Shaping favorable attitudes toward the subject matter, the instructor, learning, and education in general can have positive long-range consequences for student achievement.

Because motivation is such a critical variable in learning, it is treated in more depth here than the other nine instructional variables. On pp. 74–75 is a table entitled "Motivation for Learning." This table is an attempt to summarize the major categories of motivation schemes. Careful study of this table will show a movement toward less abstract motivational systems from one to five. You may also feel that it is necessary to make value judgments among the five categories. Typically we place the most value on the schemes described in numbers one, two, and three, and show less preference as the motivation becomes less abstract. In all of the categories, there are implications for the teacher to have some influence in motivating a student.

There is little hope in taking the position that motivation is entirely a self-generated phenomenon residing totally within the student. If one takes this position, it offers no possibilities for the teacher to shape the environment to improve motivation. In fact, whatever position one takes, it must be conceded that it is not possible to guarantee absolutely anyone's motives. Also, most people are probably operating under all of these motivation systems, depending upon the circumstances of the moment.

All of the schemes presented deal with positive or nonaversive styles. In each case, there is a positive or desired consequence following learning that motivates the student. There is no mention of the "other side of the motivation coin." This would be aversive control: motivation caused by avoidance of negative or undesirable consequences, or escape from aversive situations.

It may be that a major portion of a learner's behavior is in the form of avoidance or escape behavior. The student performs to avoid a spanking, verbal harassment, loss of privileges at home, etc. This type of motivation scheme is at times more common because it is more easily set up. We often are told what bad things will happen if we do not attend class or prepare our lessons. Detention, probation, expulsion, retention in a grade, and many other things are specified as consequences for nonperformance. We have learned well how to tell people what they *should not do,* and the consequences. We are less sophisticated in our ability to say what a student *should do,* and the positive outcomes.

Although the evidence from research is not conclusive, learning for desirable outcomes, as perceived by the learner, may be more effective than aversive control in achieving both cognitive and affective objectives.

3. Providing a Model of Terminal Performance (Mastery). When possible, learners should be shown examples of what they are to produce or do at the end of a learning experience. Imitative learning is one of the most effective procedures by which human beings acquire new behaviors. For example, providing students with sample term papers, previously completed projects, final exam papers, or demonstrations of the desired performance can dramatically facilitate learning.

4. Active Responding. At the outset of instruction learners can profit from watching or listening to someone else perform the acts to be learned, but most learners will become proficient only if they perform the acts to be learned. Thus, it is what the learner does—not what the teacher does—that determines learning. With verbal presentations (oral or written), interspersed questions can ensure that learners are attending to, and acquiring, what is intended. In learning verbal material from a textbook, most students can profit by orally reviewing (e.g., reciting out loud) what they have read while not looking at the material. The stimuli to which learners attend and the responses they make in the learning task should be matched as closely as possible to the stimuli and responses in the terminal instructional objective.

5. Guidance. Learners should be given guidance and prompting when attempting to demonstrate new behaviors to be learned. Such prompts should be eliminated gradually so the learner is able to perform the task without them. For example, verbal guidance could be given for each step in carrying out long division problems—then the verbal prompts should be eliminated gradually.

6. Practice. Opportunities should be provided for learners to use newly learned behaviors repeatedly. Since most instruction is designed to provide knowledge and skills that are to be used sometime after completing instruction, something must be done to ensure that what is learned will be retained and transferred to the postinstructional situation. Overlearning, which involves repeatedly using or practicing a newly learned behavior, can greatly facilitate retention. Practice and reviews spaced periodically after initial acquisition are also effective. With skills that are required to be performed in a variety of tasks and situations, practice should be provided in varied tasks and situations. Practice will also be more effective to the extent that the behaviors practiced are similar to behaviors to be performed in the future (the terminal objectives). For example, after initially learning to subtract, practice with a variety of number combinations should be provided.

7. Knowledge of Results. Learners should have prompt and frequent knowledge of the success of their responses. The learner must find his/her success rewarding in order for the behavior to be reinforced. Ideally, the learner should know an instant after he/she makes a response whether it is appropriate or not. When possible, the learner should be provided with the criteria to evaluate the correctness of his/her own responses. When the learner is personally confident of the correctness of his/her response, external confirmation may be unnecessary, but when he/she is unsure, such feedback is generally desirable. When a learner's response is incorrect, he/she should be informed of the correct response.

8. Graduated Sequence. Subject matter should be organized in a hierarchical form from the simple to the complex, from the familiar to the unfamiliar. The steps should be paced so that the learner succeeds in each step but does not become bored. One approach to sequencing instruction involves a careful analysis of each terminal objective, identifying the particular stimuli to which the student responds and the responses he/she is to make (see Briggs, 1968; Gagné, 1970). Then by asking what the learner must be able to do (skills, knowledge) immediately prior to performing the terminal behavior, the teacher can state another objective. The same question is then asked again and again—the teacher each time specifying objectives that are prerequisite to performing objectives at the next higher stage—until eventually the instructor arrives at the behavior with which he/she expects students to begin the course or unit. Thus, by working backwards, a sequence of enroute or intermediate objectives are identified that should lead a student from entry to mastery of the objective. (This procedure is described in more detail in chapter 3 and again in chapter 6.)

It also has been found that permitting students to follow their own sequence in achieving well-defined objectives can improve upon teacher-designed learning sequences (Mager and Clark, 1963).

9. Individual Differences. People learn at different speeds; thus, learning experiences should be designed in such a way that each student may proceed at his/her own pace. Some students will require considerable practice to master a concept, while others may acquire the same concept upon first encounter. We already have discussed one aspect of dealing with learners' individual differences in chapter 3, where we examined various methods of preassessment. Recall that preassessment involves the application of various testing procedures to assess learners' competencies before an instructional unit begins. As such, preassessment results can be used to tailor instructional units to suit the needs of individual students or groups of students. In chapter 6 we will discuss the concept of mastery learning, which also has relevance in planning instructional procedures that are designed to deal with individual differences in learners.

10. Classroom Teaching Performance. Skills in stimulating interest, explaining, guiding, identifying and administering reinforcers, and managing classroom behavior can make an enormous difference in instructional effectiveness. Unfortunately, such social skills are often the most difficult to learn, but some current work on the analysis of social and personality factors in teaching shows promise of reducing some of the complexity. The changing role of the teacher from information-dispenser to manager of instructional experiences is also an encouraging development.

SOME KEY PRINCIPLES OF INSTRUCTION

There are several distinguishable modes of instruction. The following are among the most frequently used:

1. The lecture
2. The discussion class
3. The recitation class
4. The laboratory class
5. The tutoring session
6. The demonstration

7. Independent study
8. Programed instruction
9. Reading (books, articles, etc.)
10. Motion pictures, television, filmstrips

Each of these modes can be analyzed in terms of the extent to which each of the ten principles of instruction, described previously, can be effectively applied. The result of such an analysis can then be consulted in determining which mode or combination of modes would offer the most efficient instructional procedure for achieving particular objectives. Generally speaking,

1. Prelearning preparation can be accomplished with all modes.
2. Most modes can be employed to motivate students; however, extensive use of lectures, recitation classes, and some programed instruction materials often has detrimental effects on student motivation.
3. Most modes can be used to provide a model of terminal performance— but unfortunately they are rarely used for this purpose. Demonstration is probably the most frequently used technique for showing students what they are to learn.
4. Active responding, guidance and prompting, practice and knowledge of results are rarely provided in lectures, demonstrations, and films but are usually well provided for in tutorial and programed instruction.
5. Most modes can be used in a progressive sequence of instruction, but again tutorial and programed instruction are often the most systematically sequenced modes of instruction.
6. Tutorial instruction, programed instruction, independent study, and often laboratory or studio instruction are the modes that are generally most responsive to individual differences.
7. The modes typically employed in group-paced instruction, i.e., lecture, discussion, recitation, and demonstration, usually require considerable extemporaneous ability and a high degree of social awareness. Success with more individualized modes, i.e., programed instruction and independent study, is more dependent upon a teacher's ability to select, prescribe, and evaluate the effectiveness of learning activities.

In selecting modes of instruction, the instructor should take into consideration his/her own strengths and weaknesses. For example, if an instructor is a highly stimulating speaker, it would be reasonable for him/her to give an introductory lecture to stimulate student's interest (motivation) in a new unit. On the other hand, an uninspiring speaker should probably use another means to motivate students—such as a film, a thought-provoking article, a field trip, a group discussion, or even a visiting speaker. Similarly, a teacher who has a tendency to dominate group discussions should either employ discussion procedures that exclude him/her from participating or avoid using discussions.

While the above principles apply to instruction in all behavior domains, we have included a special section that deals primarily with suggested instructional procedures for the affective domain.

SPECIAL CONSIDERATION OF INSTRUCTIONAL PROCEDURES FOR THE AFFECTIVE DOMAIN

While specific affective goals are as varied as goals pertaining to other behavior domains, instruction in the affective domain typically focuses on the establishment and/or maintenance of desirable attitudes in learners. The teacher often is concerned with establishing and/or maintaining favorable learner attitudes about the subject matter or, in some instances (e.g., social studies, sociology, and ethics), culturally determined acceptable patterns of behavior. Consequently, the teacher may find the extensive literature on the nature of attitude and attitude change useful when devising instructional procedures to achieve affective goals. The quantity and variety of literature on attitudes precludes a thorough examination of ways it can be applied to instruction in the affective domain. However, the teacher may find the following suggestions useful and is encouraged to develop additional instructional procedures based on principles found in the literature on attitudes.

Role Playing. Several studies (e.g., Janis and King, 1954; King and Janis, 1956; Culbertson, 1957; Scott, 1957, 1959; Janis and Mann, 1965; Wallace, 1966) have suggested that role playing can be an effective technique for inducing attitude change. While teachers of creative dramatics have employed role-playing and improvisation techniques for years, there appears to be potentially a much wider application of these techniques for classroom instruction. For example, there is some evidence to suggest that role playing in psychodrama can be used to modify prejudiced attitudes toward minority groups (Culbertson, 1957). Other studies provide evidence that role-playing techniques can be used to modify attitudes about alcohol (Harvey and Beverly, 1961), measures to protect one's health (Janis and Mann, 1965), and capital punishment (Wallace, 1966). Overall, the results of considerable research on attitudes suggests that various role-playing techniques can be applied to instruction in the affective domain. Moreover, role-playing techniques appear consistent with several of the previously discussed general principles related to more traditional instructional procedures, among them, motivation, active responding, and practice.

Source Credibility. Considerable research on attitudes has indicated that, in general, highly credible sources produce greater attitude change than sources low in credibility (Hovland, Janis, and Kelley, 1953; Anderson and Clevenger, 1963; McGuire, 1969). While it is reasonable to assume that the teacher is considered a credible source by most learners, there appear to be additional ways in which a teacher may employ the research findings on source credibility to achieve affective goals. For example, young children often view messages on television as being highly credible (fortunately or unfortunately!). The teacher might take advantage of this fact by employing video tapes of various popular television shows that illustrate desired affective goals. In addition, the examples provided by the video-taped messages could serve as a basis for subsequent discussion and interaction with learners about the relevant affective goals illustrated. A similar, but less expensive, instructional procedure might involve the use of popular recorded music to illustrate affective goals. Popular recording artists and their music play a significant part in most young people's lives. Consequently, music dealing with such socially relevant topics as ecology, race relations, and patriotism would appear an effective means for stimulating learners about relevant affective goals.

Other Suggestions. While a variety of research findings on attitudes may guide the teacher in developing instructional procedures for the affective domain, we are not suggesting that these research findings constitute a panacea for all of the difficulties involved with instruction related to affective goals. Moreover, we recognize that relative to other domains little attention has been given to the affective domain in terms of providing teachers with guidelines for specifying performance goals and instructional procedures. Perhaps among the few generalizations that can be made for the instructor are (1) to permit students to have as much control over what and how they learn as is feasible; (2) to try to select objectives and learning experiences that would be of interest to the students; (3) to provide learning activities that are challenging but with which a student can succeed; (4) to attempt to win the respect and affection of his/her students; and (5) to make the instructional environment as pleasant and comfortable as possible (from the student's point of view)—e.g., this would include concern for such obvious factors as temperature control, elimination of visual and auditory distractions, and use of comfortable furniture. In addition, the use of stimuli that have positive associations for the students might be introduced (e.g., inclusion of humor in instructional presentations, use of current and "relevant" examples to support a point, use of graphic and visual media in the contemporary idiom).

SUMMARY

In the first part of the chapter ten principles for designing instructional procedures were presented and discussed. These principles focused on topics such as prelearning preparation, motivation, active responding, practice, knowledge of results, and individual differences. In the last part of the chapter several modes of instruction were discussed briefly, including some instructional procedures for achieving objectives in the affective domain.

5

OBJECTIVES AND
THE BEHAVIORAL DOMAINS

After completing this chapter, the learner should be able to:

1. State at least four values of behavioral taxonomies;
2. Describe how behavioral taxonomies are related to:
   (a) specifying instructional objectives,
   (b) preassessing entry and terminal behaviors,
   (c) designing instructional procedures;
3. Describe and provide examples of the interrelationships among the three behavioral domains;
4. Specify the major levels of behavior listed in each of the three behavioral domains;
5. State or write an example of an instructional objective in his/her content area appropriate for each level of behavior listed in the cognitive, affective, and psychomotor behavioral taxonomies.

At this point we will deviate somewhat from the overall organization of the book. In the first chapter a rationale for using instructional objectives was presented, followed by an overview of the general model of instruction. In subsequent chapters we examined the first three components of the instructional model. Following this organization, you might expect the present chapter to focus on the fourth component of the instructional model. However, before turning our attention to evaluation, it will be beneficial to examine three taxonomies of learner behaviors representing the three domains of behavior with which education typically has dealt—cognitive, affective, and psychomotor. In this chapter we will examine the reasons for employing behavioral taxonomies in writing instructional objectives, discuss the interrelationships among the three behavioral domains, and present complete taxonomies for the three behavioral domains.

REASONS FOR USING BEHAVIORAL TAXONOMIES

In attempting to specify and measure instructional objectives, it is usually desirable to determine the classes of behaviors represented by the objectives. Teachers and researchers have found it useful to classify objectives into cognitive, affective, and psychomotor domains. These behavioral domains still represent only broad classifications of human behavior and educational objectives. Within each of these behavioral areas it is possible to classify objectives into progressive levels of development. Bloom and others (1956) and Krathwohl and others (1964) have conducted a systematic survey of educational objectives in the cognitive and affective domains and have prepared taxonomies for these two classes of behavior. The taxonomies evolved as a result of a 1948 meeting of university examiners and scholars interested in test development and construction at an American Psychological Association Convention in Boston. The taxonomies were prepared in response to a need expressed by members of this group for standardized terminology regarding the human behavioral characteristics that educators attempt to appraise.

Educators often are faced with the problem of interpreting abstract terms such as *like, appreciate, value, understand, enjoy,* and *know.* In the statement, "I want my students to enjoy classical music," it is unclear whether the author of the objective wants students to (1) listen to the music without throwing paper wads at other students, (2) go out and buy a classical record as a result of the course, (3) have a "deep emotional reaction" to a given piece of music, or (4) change one's major area of study to classical music. This wide range of possible variations and subsequent interpretations among educators regarding abstract objectives provided an additional stimulus for the development of the taxonomies. The taxonomies provide a framework for specifying specific objectives as well as an alternative to the common abstract statements concerning instructional goals.

It is reasonable to question the rationale for classifying rather complex behaviors into simple behavioral domains. Bloom and others (1956) suggested at least four values that provide the rationale for their taxonomies:

1. "To help clarify and tighten language of educational objectives";
2. "To provide a convenient system for describing and ordering test items, examination techniques, and evaluation instruments";
3. "To provide a framework for comparing and studying educational programs";
4. "To discover some of the principles of ordering human-learning outcomes . . . that a useful theory of learning must be able to explain."

The values of taxonomies stated above are related to the four components of the general model of instruction. In the following sections we will examine briefly how the behavioral taxonomies are related to the first three components of the model. In chapter 6 we provide examples of how the behavioral taxonomies may be used in designing evaluation procedures.

Instructional Objectives

As indicated in previous chapters, instructional objectives require teachers to specify learner performance in terms of observable, measurable behaviors. It is, of course, easier to meet this requirement for some learner behaviors than it is for others. For example, it probably would not be difficult to specify and measure the observable behaviors necessary to adjust a carburetor correctly, but it would be difficult to specify and measure the observable behaviors associated with an appreciation for classical music. Part of the ease or difficulty in specifying observable, measurable behaviors is related to the nature of the behavior with which you are concerned, that is, what type of behavior—cognitive, affective, psychomotor—is to be specified. We already have suggested that behaviors in the cognitive and psychomotor domains often are more easily specified in observable, measurable terms than behaviors in the affective domain. However, there is another issue concerning the relative ease or difficulty in specifying learner behaviors that pertains to the specific type of behavior required *within* a particular domain rather than *across* the three domains. The issue is concerned with the level of the behaviors (in terms of complexity or difficulty) as classified within each behavioral taxonomy. In general, it is less difficult to specify performance in observable, measurable terms for lower level behaviors (e.g., knowledge, awareness, physical set) than it is for higher level behaviors (e.g., synthesis, characterization, complex overt response). Of course, most units of instruction focus on several learner behaviors ranging from the very simple to the very complex. As such, it is important for teachers to specify instructional objectives for learning outcomes at all levels of difficulty. However, since it generally is less difficult to specify objectives for lower level behaviors than for higher levels, there is a tendency for instructional objective writers to over-emphasize objectives for the lower level behaviors. Incidently, this state of affairs may have prompted some critics of instructional objectives to argue that the use of instructional objectives results in trivial learner outcomes. An overemphasis on lower level behaviors is not a fault of instructional objectives; rather it is a fault of the person writing the objectives. An objective writer may avoid this pitfall if he/she uses a behavioral taxonomy when writing instructional objectives. The taxonomy will serve as a guide for the objective writer in determining (1) what is the appropriate level of behavior associated with a desired learning outcome and (2) the extent to which objectives for a unit of instruction reflect various levels of behavior. In essence, behavioral taxonomies serve to guide the objective writer in specifying the appropriate type (i.e., level) and variety of behaviors desired for given units of instruction.

Preassessment

Recall that preassessment is designed to determine (1) whether students have the prerequisite behavioral capabilities for the instruction to follow, (2) how much of what is to be learned is already known, and (3) the instructional activities that should be presented to each student. As such, preassessment procedures are directly related to the objectives for a given unit of instruction and, consequently, are related to the behaviors at various levels of the behavioral domains. In chapter 3, three types of preassessment were examined: preassessment of entry behaviors, preassessment of terminal behaviors, and preassessment for prescribing instructional procedures. Since the relationship between the behavioral taxonomies and instructional procedures will be examined in the next section, we will not discuss instructional procedures here.

In preassessment of entry behaviors the major concern is to determine whether students have the necessary prerequisite capabilities for the instruction to follow. Behavioral taxonomies may be used as guidelines for

sequentially arranging instructional objectives according to complexity
(i.e., level). Once this is accomplished, the lower level objectives may be
examined to determine what prerequisite capabilities students must have
to master them. Preassessment procedures then could be developed to
assess students' entry behavior regarding these prerequisite capabilities.

In preassessment of terminal behaviors the major concern is to determine how much of what is to be learned is already known. Behavioral
taxonomies may be used to arrange instructional objectives in the same
manner as described previously. The difference is that the hierarchical
arrangement of objectives would be used to develop preassessment measures designed to indicate which instructional objectives for a given unit
students already have mastered and which they have not. The preassessment results then could be used to determine each student's level in the
hierarchy of objectives. The results may indicate that some students
require instruction for only the higher level objectives, while other students may require instruction for low level objectives before attempting to
master higher level objectives.[1] The procedures for using a hierarchical
arrangement of objectives for preassessment and evaluation purposes are
discussed more completely in chapters 3 and 6.

Instructional Procedures

Ideally, the behavioral taxonomies could be used as guidelines to
prescribe instructional procedures designed to maximize learning for particular levels of behavior indicated in objectives. Unfortunately, research
on various instructional strategies offers no conclusive findings about
which instructional procedures are most effective for achieving given levels
of desired learner outcomes. While there is some evidence to suggest that
the lecture method is less efficient than others for producing higher level
behaviors in students, the findings are inconsistent and offer no generalized principles. Consequently, the teacher may have to rely on his/her
experience in teaching given instructional units to determine which instructional procedures appear to work best for achieving given levels of
desired learner outcomes. Even so, reference to the behavioral taxonomies
will aid the teacher in prescribing instructional procedures for given
objectives.

[1]It should be noted that a hierarchical arrangement of objectives is only applicable for content areas that are sequentially dependent. A different type of arrangement should be used for those content areas that are not sequentially dependent (see
Briggs, 1968).

INTERRELATIONSHIPS AMONG THE THREE BEHAVIORAL
DOMAINS

Some objectives include more than one behavioral domain. For example, an objective such as "to be able to present an original five-minute speech in front of the class without exhibiting stage fright" includes as many as three different domains of human behavior. The first class of behaviors implied in this objective is psychomotor skills involved in meaningful sound production; the second behavioral class involves attitudes toward the speaking situation, or affective behaviors. The objective also assumes that the student is capable of comprehending and repeating information contained in the speech (cognitive behaviors). Thus, what on the surface appears to be a simple objective of instruction involves several different classes or domains of behavior. Moreover, some classes of behavior are easier to evaluate than others. The psychomotor and cognitive aspects of the above objective would be considerably easier to evaluate objectively than the aspects dealing with attitudes.

The above example illustrates that it is often difficult to isolate the behavioral domains present in a given objective. In fact, one of the major drawbacks of the taxonomy of behaviors is the tendency to place a specific objective in one behavioral domain when it more properly should be placed in two or more of the domains. This weakness of classification systems has long been recognized. We are all familiar with the attacks by general semanticists on Aristotle for attempting to classify matter into discrete units. However, Aristotle's classifications still exist as do others in physical, biological, and social sciences as well as in education. The pragmatic values of such classification schemes often outweigh the drawbacks.

Although educators accept the fact that affective, cognitive, and psychomotor skills are interrelated highly in many areas, it often is necessary to emphasize one of the areas to the exclusion of the others in order to measure achievement of desired skills objectively. For example, an objective, "to be able to recite the Preamble to the Constitution in front of the class," generally would be placed in the cognitive domain. An educator attempting to measure this objective would no doubt listen as the student recites and note the accuracy of the recitation. However, the underlying reason for having a child recite the Preamble to the Constitution also, no doubt, would involve a less clearly defined set of objectives relating to the formation of positive attitudes towards one's cultural heritage and, specifically, one's government. These objectives relating to the affective domain would be much more difficult to measure objectively and, therefore, might be overlooked or never recognized consciously. Since recitation involves the physiological act of speech, there are also objectives related to the psychomotor domain subsumed under the original objectives. These could be measured by the instructor, if desired, but usually would not be emphasized or would be taken for granted.

Thus, even though it is virtually impossible to isolate the three behavioral domains in practice, there is still some justification for placing an objective in one of three categories from a practical viewpoint. Educators should be aware that making such arbitrary classifications of objectives could lead potentially to emphases in learning that are not necessarily most important. They should, therefore, view the following classifications of objectives with some caution.

COGNITIVE DOMAIN

When developing the taxonomies, Bloom's committee found that the majority of objectives in the educational literature was related to the cognitive domain. The objectives classified as cognitive emphasize intellectual, learning, and problem-solving tasks. Behaviors in this domain range from performing simple recall tasks to placing previously learned material into new contexts and synthesizing bodies of learned information. The following abstract of the taxonomy of educational objectives for the cognitive domain indicates the levels of cognitive behaviors under which objectives may be classified, provides brief definitions for each level, and, in most cases, provides sample objectives for the specific levels of behavior.

A CONDENSED VERSION OF THE COGNITIVE DOMAIN OF THE TAXONOMY OF EDUCATIONAL OBJECTIVES[2]

Knowledge

1.00 KNOWLEDGE

Knowledge, as defined here, involves the recall of specifics and universals, the recall of methods and processes, or the recall of a pattern,

[2]From David R. Krathwohl, Benjamin S. Bloom, and Bertram B. Masia, *Taxonomy of Educational Objectives—The Classification of Educational Goals, Hand-*

structure, or setting. For measurement purposes, the recall situation involves little more than bringing to mind the appropriate material. Although some alteration of the material may be required, this is a relatively minor part of the task. The knowledge objectives emphasize most the psychological processes of remembering. The process of relating is also involved in that a knowledge test situation requires the organization and reorganization of a problem such that it will furnish the appropriate signals and cues for the information and knowledge the individual possesses. To use an analogy, if one thinks of the mind as a file, the problem in a knowledge test situation is that of finding in the problem or task the appropriate signals, cues, and clues which will most effectively bring out whatever knowledge is filed or stored.

1.10 Knowledge of Specifics
The recall of specific and isolable bits of information. The emphasis is on symbols with concrete referents. This material, which is at a very low level of abstraction, may be thought of as the elements from which more complex and abstract forms of knowledge are built.

1.11 Knowledge of Terminology. Knowledge of the referents for specific symbols (verbal and nonverbal). This may include knowledge of the most generally accepted symbol referent, knowledge of the variety of symbols which may be used for a single referent, or knowledge of the referent most appropriate to a given use of a symbol.

To define technical terms by giving their attributes, properties, or relations.

Familiarity with a large number of words in their common range of meanings.[3]

1.12 Knowledge of Specific Facts. Knowledge of dates, events, persons, places, etc. This may include very precise and specific information such as the specific date or exact magnitude of a phenomenon. It may also include approximate or relative information such as an approximate time period or the general order of magnitude of a phenomenon.

The recall of major facts about particular cultures.

book II: Affective Domain. New York: David McKay Co., Inc., © 1964, pp. 186–193. Reprinted by permission of David McKay Co., Inc. (This is an abstract of Benjamin S. Bloom et al., *Taxonomy of Educational Objectives—The Classification of Educational Goals, Handbook I: Cognitive Domain,* New York: David McKay Co., Inc., 1956.)

[3]Each subcategory is followed by illustrative educational objectives selected from the literature.

The possession of a minimum knowledge about the organisms studied in the laboratory.

1.20 Knowledge of Ways and Means of Dealing With Specifics
Knowledge of the ways of organizing, studying, judging, and criticizing. This includes the methods of inquiry, the chronological sequences, and the standards of judgment within a field as well as the patterns of organization through which the areas of the fields themselves are determined and internally organized. This knowledge is at an intermediate level of abstraction between specific knowledge on the one hand and knowledge of universals on the other. It does not so much demand the activity of the student in using the materials as it does a more passive awareness of their nature.

1.21 Knowledge of Conventions. Knowledge of characteristic ways of treating and presenting ideas and phenomena. For purposes of communication and consistency, workers in a field employ usages, styles, practices, and forms which best suit their purposes and/or which appear to suit best the phenomena with which they deal. It should be recognized that although these forms and conventions are likely to be set up on arbitrary, accidental, or authoritative bases, they are retained because of the general agreement or concurrence of individuals concerned with the subject, phenomena, or problem.

Familiarity with the forms and conventions of the major types of works; e.g., verse, plays, scientific papers, etc.
To make pupils conscious of correct form and usage in speech and writing.

1.22 Knowledge of Trends and Sequences. Knowledge of the processes, directions, and movements of phenomena with respect to time.

Understanding of the continuity and development of American culture as exemplified in American life.
Knowledge of the basic trends underlying the development of public assistance programs.

1.23 Knowledge of Classifications and Categories. Knowledge of the classes, sets, divisions, and arrangements which are regarded as fundamental for a given subject field, purpose, argument, or problem.

To recognize the area encompassed by various kinds of problems or materials.
Becoming familiar with a range of types of literature.

1.24 Knowledge of Criteria. Knowledge of the criteria by which facts, principles, opinions, and conduct are tested or judged.

Familiarity with criteria for judgment appropriate to the type of work and the purpose for which it is read.
Knowledge of criteria for the evaluation of recreational activities.

1.25 Knowledge of Methodology. Knowledge of the methods of inquiry, techniques, and procedures employed in a particular subject field as well as those employed in investigating particular problems and phenomena. The emphasis here is on the individual's knowledge of the method rather than his ability to use the method.

Knowledge of scientific methods for evaluating health concepts.
The student shall know the methods of attack relevant to the kinds of problems of concern to the social sciences.

1.30 Knowledge of the Universals and Abstractions in a Field.
Knowledge of the major schemes and patterns by which phenomena and ideas are organized. These are the large structures, theories, and generalizations which dominate a subject field or which are quite generally used in studying phenomena or solving problems. These are at the highest levels of abstraction and complexity.

1.31 Knowledge of Principles and Generalizations. Knowledge of particular abstractions which summarize observations of phenomena. These are the abstractions which are of value in explaining, describing, predicting, or in determining the most appropriate and relevant action or direction to be taken.

Knowledge of the important principles by which our experience with biological phenomena is summarized.
The recall of major generalizations about particular cultures.

1.32 Knowledge of Theories and Structures. Knowledge of the *body* of principles and generalizations together with their interrelations which present a clear, rounded, and systematic view of a complex phenomenon, problem, or field. These are the most abstract formulations, and they can be used to show the interrelation and organization of a great range of specifics.

The recall of major theories about particular cultures.
Knowledge of a relatively complete formulation of the theory of evolution.

Intellectual Abilities and Skills

Abilities and skills refer to organized modes of operation and generalized techniques for dealing with materials and problems. The materials and problems may be of such a nature that little or no specialized and technical information is required. Such information as is required can be assumed to be part of the individual's general fund of knowledge. Other problems may require specialized and technical information at a rather high level such that specific knowledge and skill in dealing with the problem and the materials are required. The abilities and skills objectives emphasize the mental processes of organizing and reorganizing material to achieve a particular purpose. The materials may be given or remembered.

2.00 COMPREHENSION

This represents the lowest level of understanding. It refers to a type of understanding or apprehension such that the individual knows what is being communicated and can make use of the material or idea being communicated without necessarily relating it to other material or seeing its fullest implications.

2.10 Translation

Comprehension as evidenced by the care and accuracy with which the communication is paraphrased or rendered from one language or form of communication to another. Translation is judged on the basis of faithfulness and accuracy; that is, on the extent to which the material in the original communication is preserved although the form of the communication has been altered.

> The ability to understand nonliteral statements (metaphor, symbolism, irony, exaggeration).
> Skill in translating mathematical verbal material into symbolic statements and vice versa.

2.20 Interpretation

The explanation or summarization of a communication. Whereas translation involves an objective part-for-part rendering of a communication, interpretation involves a reordering, rearrangement, or new view of the material.

> The ability to grasp the thought of the work as a whole at any desired level of generality.

The ability to interpret various types of social data.

2.30 Extrapolation

The extension of trends or tendencies beyond the given data to determine implications, consequences, corollaries, effects, etc., which are in accordance with the conditions described in the original communication.

The ability to deal with the conclusions of a work in terms of the immediate inference made from the explicit statements.
Skill in predicting continuation of trends.

3.00 APPLICATION

The use of abstractions in particular and concrete situations. The abstractions may be in the form of general ideas, rules of procedures, or generalized methods. The abstractions may also be technical principles, ideas, and theories which must be remembered and applied.

Application to the phenomena discussed in one paper of the scientific terms or concepts used in other papers.
The ability to predict the probable effect of a change in a factor on a biological situation previously at equilibrium.

4.00 ANALYSIS

The breakdown of a communication into its constituent elements or parts such that the relative hierarchy of ideas is made clear and/or the relations between the ideas expressed are made explicit. Such analyses are intended to clarify the communication, to indicate how the communication is organized, and the way in which it manages to convey its effects, as well as its basis and arrangement.

4.10 Analysis of Elements
Identification of the elements included in a communication.

The ability to recognize unstated assumptions.
Skill in distinguishing facts from hypotheses.

4.20 Analysis of Relationships
The connections and interactions between elements and parts of a communication.

Ability to check the consistency of hypotheses with given information and assumptions.

Skill in comprehending the interrelationships among the ideas in a passage.

4.30 Analysis of Organizational Principles

The organization, systematic arrangement, and structure which hold the communication together. This includes the "explicit" as well as "implicit" structure. It includes the bases, necessary arrangement, and mechanics which make the communication a unit.

The ability to recognize form and pattern in literary or artistic works as a means of understanding their meaning.

Ability to recognize the general techniques used in persuasive materials, such as advertising, propaganda, etc.

5.00 SYNTHESIS

The putting together of elements and parts so as to form a whole. This involves the process of working with pieces, parts, elements, etc., and arranging and combining them in such a way as to constitute a pattern or structure not clearly there before.

5.10 Production of a Unique Communication

The development of a communication in which the writer or speaker attempts to convey ideas, feelings, and/or experiences to others.

Skill in writing, using an excellent organization of ideas and statements.

Ability to tell a personal experience effectively.

5.20 Production of a Plan, or Proposed Set of Operations

The development of a plan of work or the proposal of a plan of operations. The plan should satisfy requirements of the task which may be given to the student or which he may develop for himself.

Ability to propose ways of testing hypotheses.

Ability to plan a unit of instruction for a particular teaching situation.

5.30 Derivation of a Set of Abstract Relations

The development of a set of abstract relations either to classify or explain particular data or phenomena, or the deduction of propositions and relations from a set of basic propositions or symbolic representations.

Ability to formulate appropriate hypotheses based upon an analysis of

factors involved, and to modify such hypotheses in the light of new factors and considerations.
Ability to make mathematical discoveries and generalizations.

6.00 EVALUATION

Judgments about the value of material and methods for given purposes. Quantitative and qualitative judgments about the extent to which material and methods satisfy criteria. Use of a standard of appraisal. The criteria may be those determined by the student or those which are given to him.

6.10 Judgments in Terms of Internal Evidence
Evaluation of the accuracy of a communication from such evidence as logical accuracy, consistency, and other internal criteria.

Judging by internal standards, the ability to assess general probability of accuracy in reporting facts from the care given to exactness of statement, documentation, proof, etc.
The ability to indicate logical fallacies in arguments.

6.20 Judgments in Terms of External Criteria
Evaluation of material with reference to selected or remembered criteria.

The comparison of major theories, generalizations, and facts about particular cultures.
Judging by external standards, the ability to compare a work with the highest known standards in its field—especially with other works of recognized excellence.

AFFECTIVE DOMAIN

The second largest number of objectives found in the educational literature could be placed into one of the levels of the affective domain. The taxonomy committee found it more difficult to determine a hierarchial order of affective behaviors. The affective domain contains behaviors and objectives which have some emotional overtone. It encompasses likes and dislikes, attitudes, values and beliefs. The following is an abstract of the taxonomy of educational objectives for the affective domain.

A CONDENSED VERSION OF THE AFFECTIVE DOMAIN OF THE TAXONOMY OF EDUCATIONAL OBJECTIVES[4]

1.0 RECEIVING (ATTENDING)

At this level we are concerned that the learner be sensitized to the existence of certain phenomena and stimuli, that is, that he be willing to receive or to attend to them. This is clearly the first and crucial step if the learner is to be properly oriented to learn what the teacher intends that he will. To indicate that this is the bottom rung of the ladder, however, is not at all to imply that the teacher is starting *de novo*. Because of previous experience (formal or informal), the student brings to each situation a point of view or set which may facilitate or hinder his recognition of the phenomena to which the teacher is trying to sensitize him.

The category of *Receiving* has been divided into three subcategories to indicate three different levels of attending to phenomena. While the division points between the subcategories are arbitrary, the subcategories do represent a continuum. From an extremely passive position or role on the part of the learner, where the sole responsibility for the evocation of the behavior rests with the teacher—that is, the responsibility rests with him for "capturing" the student's attention—the continuum extends to a point at which the learner directs his attention, at least at a semiconscious level, toward the preferred stimuli.

1.1 Awareness

Awareness is almost a cognitive behavior. But unlike *Knowledge,* the lowest level of the cognitive domain, we are not so much concerned with a memory of, or ability to recall, an item or fact as we are that, given appropriate opportunity, the learner will merely be conscious of something—that he take into account a situation, phenomenon, object, or stage of affairs. Like *Knowledge* it does not imply an assessment of the qualities or nature of the stimulus, but unlike *Knowledge* it does not necessarily imply attention. There can be simple awareness without specific discrimination or recognition of the objective characteristics of the object, even

---

[4]From David R. Krathwohl, Benjamin S. Bloom, and Bertram B. Masia, *Taxonomy of Educational Objectives—The Classification of Educational Goals, Handbook II: Affective Domain.* New York: David McKay Co., Inc., © 1964, pp. 176–185. Reprinted by permission of David McKay Co., Inc.

though these characteristics must be deemed to have an effect. The individual may not be able to verbalize the aspects of the stimulus which cause the awareness.

> Develops awareness of aesthetic factors in dress, furnishings, architecture, city design, good art, and the like.
>
> Develops some consciousness of color, form, arrangement, and design in the objects and structures around him and in descriptive or symbolic representations of people, things, and situations.[5]

1.2 Willingness to Receive

In this category we have come a step up the ladder but are still dealing with what appears to be cognitive behavior. At a minimum level, we are here describing the behavior of being willing to tolerate a given stimulus, not to avoid it. Like *Awareness*, it involves a neutrality or suspended judgment toward the stimulus. At this level of the continuum the teacher is not concerned that the student seek it out, nor even, perhaps, that in an environment crowded with many other stimuli the learner will necessarily attend to the stimulus. Rather, at worst, given the opportunity to attend in a field with relatively few competing stimuli, the learner is not actively seeking to avoid it. At best, he is willing to take notice of the phenomenon and give it his attention.

> Attends (carefully) when others speak—in direct conversation, on the telephone, in audiences.
>
> Appreciation (tolerance) of cultural patterns exhibited by individuals from other groups—religious, social, political, economic, national, etc.
>
> Increase in sensitivity to human need and pressing social problems.

1.3 Controlled or Selected Attention

At a somewhat higher level we are concerned with a new phenomenon, the differentiation of a given stimulus into figure and ground at a conscious or perhaps semiconscious level—the differentiation of aspects of a stimulus which is perceived as clearly marked off from adjacent impressions. The perception is still without tension or assessment, and the student may not know the technical terms or symbols with which to describe it correctly or precisely to others. In some instances it may refer not so much to the selectivity of attention as to the control of attention,

---

[5]Illustrative objectives selected from the literature follow the description of each subcategory.

so that when certain stimuli are present they will be attended to. There is an element of the learner's controlling the attention here, so that the favored stimulus is selected and attended to despite competing and distracting stimuli.

> Listens to music with some discrimination as to its mood and meaning and with some recognition of the contributions of various musical elements and instruments to the total effect.
>
> Alertness toward human values and judgments on life as they are recorded in literature.

2.0 RESPONDING

At this level we are concerned with responses which go beyond merely attending to the phenomenon. The student is sufficiently motivated that he is not just 1.2 *Willing to attend,* but perhaps it is correct to say that he is actively attending. As a first stage in a "learning by doing" process the student is committing himself in some small measure to the phenomena involved. This is a very low level of commitment, and we would not say at this level that this was "a value of his" or that he had "such and such an attitude." These terms belong to the next higher level that we describe. But we could say that he is doing something with or about the phenomenon besides merely perceiving it, as would be true at the next level below this of 1.3 *Controlled or selected attention.*

This is the category that many teachers will find best describes their "interest" objectives. Most commonly we use the term to indicate the desire that a child become sufficiently involved in or committed to a subject, phenomenon, or activity that he will seek it out and gain satisfaction from working with it or engaging in it.

2.1 Acquiescence in Responding

We might use the word "obedience" or "compliance" to describe this behavior. As both of these terms indicate, there is a passiveness so far as the initiation of the behavior is concerned, and the stimulus calling for this behavior is not subtle. Compliance is perhaps a better term than obedience, since there is more of the element of reaction to a suggestion and less of the implication of resistance or yielding unwillingly. The student makes the response, but he has not fully accepted the necessity for doing so.

> Willingness to comply with health regulations.
>
> Obeys the playground regulations.

2.2 Willingness to Respond

The key to this level is in the term "willingness," with its implication of capacity for voluntary activity. There is the implication that the learner is sufficiently committed to exhibiting the behavior that he does so not just because of a fear of punishment, but "on his own" or voluntarily. It may help to note that the element of resistance or of yielding unwillingly, which is possibly present at the previous level, is here replaced with consent or proceeding from one's own choice.

Acquaints himself with significant current issues in international, political, social, and economic affairs through voluntary reading and discussion.

Acceptance of responsibility for his own health and for the protection of the health of others.

2.3 Satisfaction in Response

The additional element in the step beyond the *Willingness to respond* level, the consent, the assent to responding, or the voluntary response, is that the behavior is accompanied by a feeling of satisfaction, an emotional response, generally of pleasure, zest, or enjoyment. The location of this category in the hierarchy has given us a great deal of difficulty. Just where in the process of internalization the attachment of an emotional response, kick, or thrill to a behavior occurs has been hard to determine. For that matter there is some uncertainty as to whether the level of internalization at which it occurs may not depend on the particular behavior. We have even questioned whether it should be a category. If our structure is to be a hierarchy, then each category should include the behavior in the next level below it. The emotional component appears gradually through the range of internalization categories. The attempt to specify a given position in the hierarchy as *the* one at which the emotional component is added is doomed to failure.

The category is arbitrarily placed at this point in the hierarchy where it seems to appear most frequently and where it is cited as, or appears to be, an important component of the objectives at this level on the continuum. The category's inclusion at this point serves the pragmatic purpose of reminding us of the presence of the emotional component and its value in the building of affective behaviors. But it should not be thought of as appearing and occurring at this one point in the continuum and thus destroying the hierarchy which we are attempting to build.

Enjoyment of self-expression in music and in arts and crafts as another means of personal enrichment.

Finds pleasure in reading for recreation.

Takes pleasure in conversing with many different kinds of people.

3.0 VALUING

This is the only category headed by a term which is in common use in the expression of objectives by teachers. Further, it is employed in its usual sense: that a thing, phenomenon, or behavior has worth. This abstract concept of worth is in part a result of the individual's own valuing or assessment, but it is much more a social product that has been slowly internalized or accepted and has come to be used by the student as his own criterion of worth.

Behavior categorized at this level is sufficiently consistent and stable to have taken on the characteristics of a belief or an attitude. The learner displays this behavior with sufficient consistency in appropriate situations that he comes to be perceived as holding a value. At this level, we are not concerned with the relationships among values but rather with the internalization of a set of specified, ideal, values. Viewed from another standpoint, the objectives classified here are the prime stuff from which the conscience of the individual is developed into active control of behavior.

This category will be found appropriate for many objectives that use the term "attitude" (as well as, of course, "value").

An important element of behavior characterized by *Valuing* is that it is motivated, not by the desire to comply or obey, but by the individual's commitment to the underlying value guiding the behavior.

3.1 Acceptance of a Value

At this level we are concerned with the ascribing of worth to a phenomenon, behavior, object, etc. The term "belief," which is defined as "the emotional acceptance of a proposition or doctrine upon what one implicitly considers adequate ground" (English and English, 1958, p. 64), describes quite well what may be thought of as the dominant characteristic here. Beliefs have varying degrees of certitude. At this lowest level of *Valuing* we are concerned with the lowest levels of certainty; that is, there is more of a readiness to re-evaluate one's position than at the higher levels. It is a position that is somewhat tentative.

One of the distinguishing characteristics of this behavior is consistency of response to the class of objects, phenomena, etc., with which the belief or attitude is identified. It is consistent enough so that the person is perceived by others as holding the belief or value. At the level we are describing here, he is both sufficiently consistent that others can identify the value and sufficiently committed that he is willing to be so identified.

Continuing desire to develop the ability to speak and write effectively.
Grows in his sense of kinship with human beings of all nations.

3.2 Preference for a Value

The provision for this subdivision arose out of a feeling that there were objectives that expressed a level of internalization between the mere acceptance of a value and commitment or conviction in the usual connotation of deep involvement in an area. Behavior at this level implies not just the acceptance of a value to the point of being willing to be identified with it, but the individual is sufficiently committed to the value to pursue it, to seek it out, to want it.

Assumes responsibility for drawing reticent members of a group into conversation.
Deliberately examines a variety of viewpoints on controversial issues with a view to forming opinions about them.
Actively participates in arranging for the showing of contemporary artistic efforts.

3.3 Commitment

Belief at this level involves a high degree of certainty. The ideas of "conviction" and "certainty beyond a shadow of a doubt" help to convey further the level of behavior intended. In some instances this may border on faith, in the sense of it being a firm emotional acceptance of a belief upon admittedly nonrational grounds. Loyalty to a position, group, or cause would also be classified here.

The person who displays behavior at this level is clearly perceived as holding the value. He acts to further the thing valued in some way, to extend the possibility of his developing it, to deepen his involvement with it and with the things representing it. He tries to convince others and seeks converts to his cause. There is a tension here which needs to be satisfied; action is the result of an aroused need or drive. There is a real motivation to act out the behavior.

Devotion to those ideas and ideals which are the foundations of democracy.
Faith in the power of reason and in methods of experiment and discussion.

4.0 ORGANIZATION

As the learner successively internalizes values, he encounters situations for which more than one value is relevant. Thus necessity arises for (a) the organization of the values into a system, (b) the determination of the interrelationships among them, and (c) the establishment of the dominant and pervasive ones. Such a system is built gradually, subject to change as new values are incorporated. This category is intended as the proper classification for objectives which describe the beginnings of the building of a value system. It is subdivided into two levels, since a prerequisite to interrelating is the conceptualization of the value in a form which permits organization. *Conceptualization* forms the first subdivision in the organization process, *Organization of a value system* the second.

While the order of the two subcategories seems appropriate enough with reference to one another, it is not so certain that 4.1 *Conceptualization of a value* is properly placed as the next level above 3.3 *Commitment*. Conceptualization undoubtedly begins at an earlier level for some objectives. Like 2.3 *Satisfaction in response,* it is doubtful that a single completely satisfactory location for this category can be found. Positioning it before 4.2 *Organization of a value system* appropriately indicates a prerequisite of such a system. It also calls attention to a component of affective growth that occurs at least by this point on the continuum but may begin earlier.

4.1 Conceptualization of a Value

In the previous category, 3.0 *Valuing,* we noted that consistency and stability are integral characteristics of the particular value or belief. At this level (4.1) the quality of abstraction or conceptualization is added. This permits the individual to see how the value relates to those that he already holds or to new ones that he is coming to hold.

Conceptualization will be abstract, and in this sense it will be symbolic. But the symbols need not be verbal symbols. Whether conceptualization first appears at this point on the affective continuum is a moot point, as noted above.

Attempts to identify the characteristics of an art object which he admires.

Forms judgments as to the responsibility of society for conserving human and material resources.

4.2 Organization of a Value System

Objectives properly classified here are those which require the learner to bring together a complex of values, possibly disparate values, and to bring these into an ordered relationship with one another. Ideally, the ordered relationship will be one which is harmonious and internally consistent. This is, of course, the goal of such objectives, which seek to have the student formulate a philosophy of life. In actuality, the integration may be something less than entirely harmonious. More likely the relationship is better described as a kind of dynamic equilibrium which is, in part, dependent upon those portions of the environment which are salient at any point in time. In many instances the organization of values may result in their synthesis into a new value or value complex of a higher order.

Weighs alternative social policies and practices against the standards of the public welfare rather than the advantage of specialized and narrow interest groups.

Develops a plan for regulating his rest in accordance with the demands of his activities.

5.0 CHARACTERIZATION BY A VALUE OR VALUE COMPLEX

At this level of internalization the values already have a place in the individual's value hierarchy, are organized into some kind of internally consistent system, have controlled the behavior of the individual for a sufficient time that he has adapted to behaving this way; and an evocation of the behavior no longer arouses emotion or affect except when the individual is threatened or challenged.

The individual acts consistently in accordance with the values he has internalized at this level, and our concern is to indicate two things: (a) the generalization of this control to so much of the individual's behavior that he is described and characterized as a person by these pervasive controlling tendencies, and (b) the integration of these beliefs, ideas, and attitudes into a total philosophy or world view. These two aspects constitute the subcategories.

5.1 Generalized Set

The generalized set is that which gives an internal consistency to the system of attitudes and values at any particular moment. It is selective responding at a very high level. It is sometimes spoken of as a determining tendency, an orientation toward phenomena, or a predisposition to act in a certain way. The generalized set is a response to highly generalized phenomena. It is a persistent and consistent response to a family of related situations or objects. It may often be an unconscious set which guides action without conscious forethought. The generalized set may be thought of as closely related to the idea of an attitude cluster, where the commonality is based on behavioral characteristics rather than the subject or object of the attitude. A generalized set is a basic orientation which enables the individual to reduce and order the complex world about him and to act consistently and effectively in it.

> Readiness to revise judgments and to change behavior in the light of evidence.

> Judges problems and issues in terms of situations, issues, purposes, and consequences involved rather than in terms of fixed, dogmatic precepts or emotionally wishful thinking.

5.2 Characterization

This, the peak of the internalization process, includes those objectives which are broadest with respect both to the phenomena covered and to the range of behavior which they comprise. Thus, here are found those objectives which concern one's view of the universe, one's philosophy of life, one's *Weltanschauung*—a value system having as its object the whole of what is known or knowable.

Objectives categorized here are more than generalized sets in the sense that they involve a greater inclusiveness and, within the group of attitudes, behaviors, beliefs, or ideas, an emphasis on internal consistency. Though this internal consistency may not always be exhibited behaviorally by the students toward whom the objective is directed, since we are categorizing teachers' objectives, this consistency feature will always be a component of *Characterization* objectives.

As the title of the category implies, these objectives are so encompassing that they tend to characterize the individual almost completely.

> Develops for regulation of one's personal and civic life a code of behavior based on ethical principles consistent with democratic ideals.

> Develops a consistent philosophy of life.

PSYCHOMOTOR DOMAIN

Bloom's committee did not develop a taxonomy for the psychomotor domain. Moreover, until recently little work had been done in this area. Below is an example of one of the more recent developments in the construction of a taxonomy for behaviors in the psychomotor domain.

BRANCHING OPTION THREE

At this point you may find it beneficial to turn to Appendix C. There you will find a brief article designed to show you how specific objectives may be formulated within the hierarchy of the major levels and sublevels of the taxonomies of educational objectives as set forth by Bloom et al., (1956) and Krathwohl et al., (1964).

THE CLASSIFICATION OF EDUCATIONAL OBJECTIVES IN THE PSYCHOMOTOR DOMAIN[6]

The major organizational principle operating is that of complexity with attention to the sequence involved in the performance of a motor act. That is, objectives that would be classified at the lower levels are less complex in nature than related objectives at upper levels. In general, they are easier to carry out. And, those at the upper levels build on those at the lower.

1.00 PERCEPTION This is an essential first step in performing a motor act. It is the process of becoming aware of objects, qualities, or relations by way of the sense organs. It is a necessary but not sufficient condition for motor activity. It is basic in the situation-interpretation-action chain leading to motor activity. The category of perception has been divided into three subcategories indicating three different levels of the perception process. This level is a parallel of the first category, receiving or attending, in the affective domain.

1.10 Sensory Stimulation—Impingement of a stimulus upon one or more of the sense organs.

1.11 Auditory Hearing or the sense of organs of hearing.

[6]From Elizabeth Jane Simpson, "The Classification of Educational Objectives in the Psychomotor Domain," *The Psychomotor Domain,* Vol. 3. Copyright © 1972 by Gryphon House, pp. 43–56. Reprinted by permission of the author.

1.12 Visual Concerned with the mental pictures or images obtained through the eyes.
1.13 Tactile Pertaining to the sense of touch.
1.14 Taste Determine the relish or flavor of by taking a portion into the mouth.
1.15 Smell To perceive by excitation of the olfactory nerves.
1.16 Kinesthetic The muscle sense; pertaining to sensitivity from activation of receptors in muscles, tendons, and joints.

1.10 Sensory Stimulation—Illustrative educational objectives.
Sensitivity to auditory cues in playing a musical instrument as a member of a group.
Awareness of difference in "hand" of various fabrics.
Sensitivity to flavors in seasoning food.

The preceding categories are not presented in any special order of importance, although, in Western cultures, the visual cues are said to have dominance, whereas in some cultures, the auditory and tactile cues may pre-empt the high position we give the visual. Probably no sensible ordering of these is possible at this time. It should also be pointed out that "the cues that guide action may change for a particular motor activity as learning progresses (e.g., kinesthetic cues replacing visual cues)."[7]

1.20 CUE SELECTION Deciding to what cues one must respond in order to satisfy the particular requirements of task performance. This involves identification of the cue or cues and associating them with the task to be performed.
It may involve grouping of cues in terms of past experience and knowledge. Cues relevant to the situation are selected as a guide to action; irrelevant cues are ignored or discarded.

1.20 Cue Selection—Illustrative educational objectives.
Recognition of operating difficulties with machinery through the sound of the machine in operation.
Sensing where the needle should be set in beginning machine stitching.

[7] Loree, Ray, Correspondence with investigator, June, 1965.

Recognizing factors to take into account in batting in a softball game.

1.30 Translation—Relating of perception to action in performing a motor act. This is the mental process of determining the meaning of the cues received for action. It involves symbolic translation, that is, having an image or being reminded of something, "having an idea," as a result of cues received. It may involve insight which is essential in solving a problem through perceiving the relationships essential to solution. Sensory translation is an aspect of this level. It involves "feedback," that is, knowledge of the effects of the process. Translation is a continuous part of the motor act being performed.

1.30 Translation—Illustrative educational objectives.
Ability to relate music to dance form.
Ability to follow a recipe in preparing food.
Knowledge of the "feel" of operating a sewing machine successfully and use of this knowledge as a guide in stitching.

2.00 SET Set is a preparatory adjustment or readiness for a particular kind of action or experience.
Three aspects of set have been identified: mental, physical, and emotional.

2.10 Mental set—Readiness, in the mental sense, to perform a certain motor act. This involves, as prerequisite, the level of perception and its subcategories. Discrimination, that is, using judgment in making distinctions, is an aspect of mental set.

2.10 Mental set—Illustrative educational objectives.
Knowledge of steps in setting the table.
Knowledge of tools appropriate to performance of various sewing operations.

2.20 Physical set—Readiness in the sense of having made the anatomical adjustments necessary for a motor act to be performed. Readiness, in the physical sense, involves receptor set, that is, sensory attending, or focusing the attention of the needed sensory organs and postural set, or positioning of the body.

2.20 Physical set—Illustrative educational objectives.
Achievement of bodily stance preparatory to bowling.
Positioning of hands preparatory to typing.

2.30 Emotional set—Readiness in terms of attitudes favorable to the motor acts taking place. Willingness to respond is implied.

2.30 Emotional set—Illustrative educational objectives
Disposition to perform sewing machine operation to best of ability.
Desire to operate a production drill press with skill.

3.00 GUIDED RESPONSE This is an early step in the development of skill. Emphasis here is upon the abilities which are components of the more complex skill. Guided response is the overt behavioral act of an individual under the guidance of the instructor or in response to self-evaluation where the student has a model or criteria against which he can judge his performance. Prerequisites to performance of the act are readiness to respond, in terms of set to produce the overt behavioral act and selection of the appropriate response. Selection of response may be defined as deciding what response must be made in order to satisfy the requirements of task performance. There appear to be two major subcategories, imitation and trial and error.

3.10 Imitation—Imitation is the execution of an act as a direct response to the perception of another person performing the act.

3.10 Imitation—Illustrative educational objectives.
Imitation of the process of stay-stitching the curved neck edge of a bodice.
Performing a dance step as demonstrated.
Debeaking a chick in the manner demonstrated.

3.20 Trial and error—Trying various responses, usually with some rationale for each response, until an appropriate response is achieved. The appropriate response is one which meets the requirements of task performance, that is, "gets the job done" or does it more efficiently. This level may be defined as multiple-response learning in which the proper response is selected out of varied behavior, possibly through the influence of reward and punishment.

3.20 Trial and error—Illustrative educational objectives.
Discovering the most efficient method of ironing a blouse through trial of various procedures.
Determining the sequence for cleaning a room through trial of several patterns.

4.00 MECHANISM Learned response has become habitual. At this level, the learner has achieved a certain confidence and degree of proficiency in the performance of the act. The act is a part of his repertoire of possible responses to stimuli and the demands of situations where the response is an appropriate one. The response may be more complex than at the preceding level; it may involve some patterning in carrying out the task.

4.00 Mechanism—Illustrative educational objectives.
Ability to perform a hand-hemming operation.
Ability to mix ingredients for butter cake.
Ability to pollinate an oat flower.

5.00 COMPLEX OVERT RESPONSE At this level, the individual can perform a motor act that is considered complex because of the movement pattern required. At this level, skill has been attained. The act can be carried out smoothly and efficiently, that is, with minimum expenditure of time and energy. There are two subcategories: resolution of uncertainty and automatic performance.

5.10 Resolution of uncertainty—The act is performed without hesitation of the individual to get a mental picture of task sequence. That is, he knows the sequence required and so proceeds with confidence. The act is here defined as complex in nature.

5.10 Resolution of uncertainty—Illustrative educational objectives.
Skill in operating a milling machine.
Skill in setting up and operating a production band saw.

5.20 Automatic performance—At this level, the individual can perform a finely coordinated motor skill with a great deal of ease and muscle control.

5.20 Automatic performance—Illustrative educational objectives.
Skill in performing basic steps of national folk dances.
Skill in tailoring a suit.
Skill in performing on the violin.

6.00 ADAPTATION Altering motor activities to meet the demands of new problematic situations requiring a physical response.

6.00 Adaptation—Illustrative educational objectives.
Developing a modern dance composition through adapting known abilities and skills in dance.

7.00 ORIGINATION Creating new motor acts or ways of manipulating materials out of understandings, abilities, and skills developed in the psychomotor area.

7.00 Origination—Illustrative educational objectives.
Creation of a modern dance.
Creation of a new game requiring psychomotor response.

SUMMARY

In the first part of this chapter a number of reasons for using behavioral taxonomies were presented. The following were listed as the specific values of behavioral taxonomies:

1. "To help clarify and tighten language of educational objectives";
2. "To provide a convenient system for describing and ordering test items, examination techniques, and evaluation instruments";
3. "To provide a framework for comparing and studying educational programs";
4. "To discover some of the principles of ordering human-learning outcomes ... that a useful theory of learning must be able to explain."

The discussion then focused on specific ways in which behavioral taxonomies are related to the instructional objectives, preassessment, and instructional procedures. A few suggestions were offered as to how one might use behavioral taxonomies as guidelines for making decisions and developing procedures relevant to the first three components of the general model of instruction. Following this material was a discussion of the interrelationships among the three behavioral domains. Although it is often virtually impossible to isolate the three behavioral domains in practice, it was concluded that there still is some justification for placing an objective in one of the three categories from a practical viewpoint. Three taxonomies, one for each behavioral domain, were then presented along with corresponding objectives for each behavior level of each domain.

6

EVALUATION

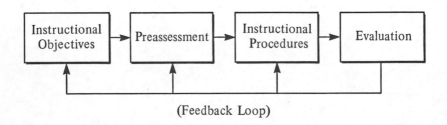

| Instructional Objectives | → | Preassessment | → | Instructional Procedures | → | Evaluation |

(Feedback Loop)

After completing this chapter, the learner should be able to:

1. State the primary purpose of evaluation;
2. Distinguish between a norm-referenced and criterion-referenced evaluation system;
3. Describe the steps in implementing a criterion-referenced evaluation system:
   a. State why behavior taxonomies should be used in specifying instructional objectives,
   b. Describe Gagné's method of behavioral analysis,
   c. Describe how appropriate evaluation procedures may be selected to assess students' mastery of instructional objectives,
   d. Describe what is meant by matching evaluation procedures to instructional objectives;
4. Identify and describe four selected problems in implementing a criterion-referenced evaluation system;
5. Describe the logic of a mastery learning system;
6. Compare and contrast the mastery learning system with the traditional system;

7. Distinguish between a mastery learning system and a modified mastery learning system;

8. Describe three alternative procedures that may be used to translate student performance within a modified mastery learning system to a system requiring student performance to be expressed in terms of graduated grades;

9. Describe a grading procedure within a modified mastery learning system that is an alternative to a grading procedure that relies on a cumulative point system or average grade system.

As suggested by the feedback loop in the general model of instruction, the primary purpose of evaluation is to assess the effectiveness of instruction. Of course, the focus of evaluation is to determine whether students achieved mastery of the instructional objectives. The evaluation procedures suggested by the general model of instruction are in some ways quite different from procedures of evaluation suggested in more traditional models of instruction. Consequently, we have devoted more space to a discussion of evaluation than to other components of the model with the possible exception of instructional objectives. In this chapter we will examine the differences between norm-referenced evaluation and criterion-referenced evaluation and the procedures for implementing a criterion-referenced evaluation system. We also will examine the concept of mastery learning and how it can be applied to evaluation and grading procedures in a modified mastery-learning system.

NORM-REFERENCED VS. CRITERION-REFERENCED EVALUATION

Current discussions about evaluation among educators often involve a comparison of norm-referenced and criterion-referenced evaluation procedures. Teachers are most familiar with norm-referenced evaluation procedures designed to ascertain a student's performance in relation to the performance of other students on the same test. This type of evaluation procedure is referred to as "norm-referenced" because an individual's performance is compared with that of a normative group (Popham and Husek, 1969). Critical to the norm-referenced procedure is the concept of relative standard—i.e., the standard performance is relative to how other individuals performed on the test. For example, a relative standard might indicate that a student correctly punctuated more sentences than other students, but it does not indicate whether the student punctuated all of the test sentences, 80 percent of them, or 20 percent of them.

Criterion-referenced evaluation procedures are designed to determine whether a student has achieved mastery of a behavior as specified in an instructional objective(s). Both the norm-referenced and criterion-referenced procedures sort students on the basis of performance, but there is an essential difference. In criterion-referenced evaluation procedures the interpretation of a student's performance is in no way dependent upon the performance of other students. Moreover, the criterion-referenced procedure assumes that if performance goals (i.e., instructional objectives) are important, teachers should be concerned with whether the student has achieved them, not with how much the student achieved relative to his/her peers (Airasian and Madaus, 1972).

The concept of criterion-referenced evaluation is not entirely new to educators. Thorndike (1918) made reference to the basic distinction between the two types of evaluation procedures, but he did not use the terms *norm-referenced* and *criterion-referenced* in his distinction. Glaser (1963) provided the initial conceptual clarity and practical implications of the two evaluation procedures that has stimulated numerous articles and papers elaborating on the applications, advantages, and liabilities of the two approaches. Table 2 provides a summary of the various statements that have been made comparing norm-referenced and criterion-referenced evaluation systems.

Two additional distinctions between norm-referenced and criterion-referenced evaluation procedures are noteworthy. These distinctions are related to *when* tests are given and *how* test results are used (Airasian and Madaus, 1972). In a norm-referenced system tests usually are given to students at the end of an instructional unit for grading purposes. In a criterion-referenced system tests ideally are used for at least four different types of testing purposes. First, criterion-referenced tests may be used for preassessment purposes (see chapter 3). Second, criterion-referenced tests may be used for formative testing (Bloom, Hastings, and Madaus, 1971)— that is, testing that is used concurrently with instruction for the purposes of checking the progress of students so that assistance may be provided when necessary. Third, criterion-referenced tests may be used to determine whether components of the instructional model (e.g., instructional objectives, instructional procedures) need modification. Fourth, criterion-referenced tests may be used at the end of an instructional unit to determine whether students have achieved the criterion levels of objectives.

TABLE 2. Comparison of General Characteristics of Norm-Referenced and Criterion-Referenced Evaluation Systems

Norm-Referenced System	Criterion-Referenced System
1. The main function of norm-referenced evaluation is to ascertain the student's relative position within a normative group.	1. The main function of criterion-referenced evaluation is to assess whether the student has mastered a specific criterion or performance standard.
2. Either general conceptual outcomes (usually done) or precise objectives may be specified when constructing norm-referenced evaluation.	2. Complete instructional objectives are specified in the construction of criterion-referenced evaluation.
3. The criterion for mastery is not usually specified when using norm-referenced evaluation.	3. The criterion for mastery must be stated (i.e., instructional objectives) for use in criterion-referenced evaluation.
4. Test items for norm-referenced evaluation are constructed to discriminate among students.	4. Test items for criterion-referenced evaluation are constructed to measure a predetermined level of proficiency.
5. Variability of scores is desirable as an aid to meaningful interpretation.	5. Variability is irrelevant; it is not a necessary condition for a satisfactory criterion-referenced evaluation.
6. The test results from norm-referenced evaluation are amenable to transposition to the traditional grading system (A, B, C, D, F).	6. The test results from criterion-referenced evaluation suggest the use of a binary system (i.e., satisfactory-unsatisfactory; pass-fail). However, criterion-referenced evaluation test results can be transposed into the traditional grading system by following a set of specifically constructed rules.

From Mary-Jeanette Smythe, Robert J. Kibler, and Patricia W. Hutchings, "A Comparison of Norm-Referenced and Criterion-Referenced Measurement with Implications for Communication Instruction," *The Speech Teacher* 22, 1973, 4. Reprinted by permission of the authors and the Speech Communication Association.

IMPLEMENTING A CRITERION-REFERENCED EVALUATION SYSTEM

The first step in implementing a criterion-referenced evaluation system is to prepare, prior to instruction, a set of instructional objectives. Most teachers will find that one or more of the taxonomies discussed in chapter 5 will provide valuable assistance in determining what specific types of performance goals should be specified to describe the skills and competencies necessary for mastery of a particular unit of instruction. We recommend that a taxonomy (or taxonomies) be used for this purpose to avoid overemphasis of performance goals that correspond to the lower level skills (e.g., knowledge, awareness, perception), for which instructional objectives often are most easily written. Reference to various behavior taxonomies will provide guidelines to insure that instructional objectives are prepared for any necessary higher level skills and competencies (e.g., synthesis, valuing, complex overt responses) required for mastery of the instructional unit.

The teacher may also find Gagné's (1970) behavioral analysis (also called task analysis) technique useful in preparing objectives for instructional units that primarily focus on complex cognitive or psychomotor skills. Gagné maintains that mastery of subordinate skills is necessary before mastery of superordinate skills can be achieved. Certainly this idea is not new—all teachers know that one must master basics before more advanced tasks can be mastered. However, Gagné does provide a unique and useful method for determining what are the necessary prerequisite skills for a given terminal objective. The method, called behavioral analysis, is accomplished by beginning with the terminal objective for a unit of instruction (e.g., the student will be able to solve simultaneous equations) and working "downward" to the necessary behaviors for the unit of instruction. This can be accomplished by successfully asking: What must a student already know how to do in order to learn this skill? The answers to these questions form the set of prerequisite skills, each of which is necessary for mastery of the terminal objective. The results of the behavioral analysis often are arranged hierarchically, with the terminal objective placed at the top position, the necessary entry behaviors at the bottommost position, and the succeeding subordinate skills at various levels in between. For example, Figure 4 is a tentative learning hierarchy for an

Figure 4 is from Judy L. Haynes, "Improving Instruction in Speech-Communication Skills Through Learning Hierarchies: An Application to Organization," *The Speech Teacher*, 22, 1973, 241. Reprinted by permission of the author and the Speech Communication Association.

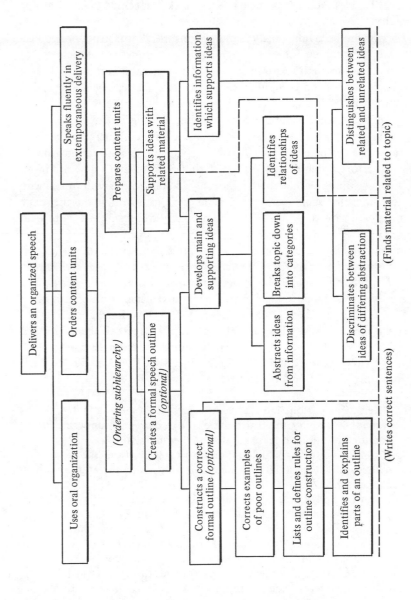

FIGURE 4. *Hierarchy of Organizational Skills*

119

instructional unit on organizing a speech. Finally, one or more instructional objectives are then prepared for each skill specified in the learning hierarchy.

Clearly the behavioral analysis method insures that instructional objectives will be specified for each type of skill or competency necessary for mastery of an instructional unit. However, the method is most applicable to units of instruction containing subject matter that can be sequenced in a hierarchical fashion and that focuses on complex cognitive or psychomotor skills. Also, development of a valid learning hierarchy for most subject areas is not an easy task. It often requires considerable time and revisions, but the benefits gained from such an analysis are commensurate with the effort it requires. We suggest that those persons who are interested in developing learning hierarchies should collaborate with others who are teaching the same content. Several persons working on the same hierarchy will save time and effort and probably will result in a more valid hierarchy.

After objectives are prepared for the unit of instruction, *the second step in implementing a criterion-referenced evaluation system is the selection of appropriate evaluation procedures to assess students' mastery of stated objectives.* While some form of paper and pencil test is most often used by teachers to assess students' mastery of instructional goals, it is not the only method of evaluation. The appropriateness of the evaluation procedure(s) selected will largely be determined by the nature of the skill or competency specified in instructional objectives. For example, consider the following instructional objectives:

1. Given 20 equations in negative integers with a missing factor, the student will apply the distributive rule in correctly supplying the missing addend in at least 18 of the 20 equations.
2. Given 20 sentences which contain no capitalization, the student will rewrite at least 18 sentences correctly, using the appropriate capitalization.
3. Given no books, notes, or other reference materials, the student will engage in a five-minute conversation in French with the teacher about one of the following topics: a hobby of mine, my family, last summer's vacation. Performance will be evaluated on the extent to which the student pronounces the words correctly, forms grammatical sentences, and expresses thoughts clearly.
4. Given complete freedom to select a topic of investigation of his/her choice, the student will design, execute, and write a report of an experiment that meets the following criteria: there

must be at least one testable hypothesis, the design must contain at least two factors of internal validity and one factor of external validity, and the results must be analyzed using at least one statistical test.

Mastery of the first two objectives would appear to be most easily assessed by some form of a paper and pencil test that the student would be required to take during a specified period of time in the classroom. The third objective clearly suggests that an oral-type testing procedure is most appropriate for assessing the critical skills specified in the objective, while the fourth objective suggests that a term paper might serve as an appropriate mode of evaluation. Of course, each of these objectives could be rewritten to suggest a different type of evaluation procedure, depending upon the level or type of skill/competence the teacher desires students to demonstrate. It should be clear that the teacher has considerable flexibility in selecting an evaluation procedure appropriate for assessing the particular level and type of performance indicated in instructional objectives.

The third step in implementing a criterion-referenced evaluation system is to match the particular evaluation procedure selected with the performance behaviors delineated in instructional objectives. It is important that the evaluation procedure(s) corresponds to the level and type of behavior(s) specified in instructional objectives; otherwise the objectives can be misleading and of little use to students, and/or the evaluation procedure(s) will not clearly indicate whether students have mastered the instructional objectives. Of course, either of these latter conditions is undesirable from both a teacher's and a student's standpoint. For example, consider the following instructional objectives and test items:

Objective: Given a diagram of a plant cell, the student will label in writing each of the five major components of a plant cell.

Test Item: Below is a diagram of a plant cell. Describe how each component of the plant cell contributes to the life of the plant and how each component interacts with other components in the cell.

Are the instructional objective and test item matched? Clearly not. The objective indicates that students should be able to identify the major components of a plant cell by labeling each component. The test item requires students to demonstrate a much higher (i.e., more sophisticated) level of behavior—i.e., describe the interrelationship and function of each component. Consequently, the objective does not clearly indicate to students the level of performance they will be expected to demonstrate. Moreover, while the test item may assess students' ability to identify and label the components of a plant cell, it is likely that the majority of students would not perform well on the test item if they only mastered the level of competency indicated in the objective. The teacher has at least two options available for correcting mismatching of this nature. The teacher can either rewrite the test item to match the objective or rewrite the objective to match the test item. For example:

> *Objective:* Given a diagram of a plant cell, the student will label in writing each of the five major components of a plant cell.
> *Test Item:* Below is a diagram of a plant cell. Label each of the five major components of the cell.

> OR

> *Objective:* Given a diagram of a plant cell, the student will label each of the five major components of the cell and describe in writing how each component contributes to the life of the plant and how it interrelates with other components.
> *Test Item:* Below is a diagram of a plant cell. Label each of the five major components of a plant cell and describe how each component: (1) contributes to the life of the plant and (2) interrelates with each of the other components.

In the preceding mismatched example, the test item required students to demonstrate a higher level of behavior than what was indicated in the instructional objective. Mismatching also can occur in the opposite direction—i.e., the test item can assess students' competency at a lower level than is indicated in the instructional objective. For example:

> *Objective:* Given one hour and no reference materials, the student will describe and synthesize in writing the series of major events leading and contributing to the United States' involvement in World War I. The product should reflect the relevant material presented in the textbook and class discussion.
> *Test Item:* List the major events that led and contributed to the United States' involvement in World War I.

In the above example the test item requires students only to list the major events, which is a considerably lower level behavior than indicated in the instructional objective. The objective indicates that students should be able to describe and synthesize the major events—e.g., write a well-organized essay. Mismatching of this type also is undesirable, particularly from the teacher's standpoint. Clearly the above test item does not assess students' mastery of the instructional objective. In this particular example most students probably would perform well on the test item, but their performance would not indicate the degree to which they were able to synthesize, integrate, and clearly express ideas relating to the major events that led to the United States' involvement in World War I. Consequently, it would be possible for students to perform well on the test item without having mastered the level of skill/competency indicated in the instructional objective. Of course, mismatching of this nature also may be corrected by either rewriting the instructional objective or rewriting the test item. However, the teacher will find that the two types of mismatching discussed can be avoided if a behavior taxonomy is used in preparing instructional objectives and in preparing corresponding test items.

To this point we have discussed and illustrated only one type of evaluation procedure—i.e., in-class paper and pencil-type test items. However, as indicated earlier in the chapter, instructional objectives are amenable to a wide variety of evaluation procedures. The general rule of matching evaluation procedures with instructional objectives applies to whatever specific evaluation procedure is used to assess students' mastery of stated objectives. Below are examples of instructional objectives matched to various types of evaluation procedures for different levels of behavior across the three behavior domains.

Cognitive Domain

1. Comprehension

Objective: Given ten questions presented orally in Russian, the student will orally answer each question in English. Performance will be evaluated on completeness of the English responses.

Evaluation Procedure: The objective suggests that an oral testing situation is most appropriate for assessment of student performance concerning this objective. The testing procedure may involve a direct one-to-one interaction between student and teacher, peer evaluations, or if the appropriate equipment is available, tape recordings may be used.

2. Analysis

Objective: Given a description of a person's attitudes about a person, object, or event, the student will select from a list of four alternatives the attitude function that is most accurately illustrated by the person's attitude.

Evaluation Procedure: The wording of this particular objective suggests that it can be matched to a multiple-choice test item. An illustrative test item might be:

> Read the following passage and select the attitude function below that is *most accurately* illustrated in the event:
>
> Tom has an inferiority complex resulting from his father's constantly harassing him about the need to "pick himself up by the bootstraps" and make a name for himself. Unfortunately for Tom, he is not very successful as an adult in terms of status, occupation, and socioeconomic position. Tom is very bitter and has developed very negative attitudes about underprivileged people that have served to help him view himself as superior.
>
> A. Adjustment Function
> B. Ego-Defensive Function
> C. Value-Expressive Function
> D. Knowledge Function

3. Evaluation

Objective: Given one week, the student will select an experimental study reported in a journal of his/her choosing and write a five-page paper in which the theoretical and methodological worth of the study is evaluated. The product will be evaluated on the extent to which it reflects the criteria for evaluation of experimental research supplied to the student.

Evaluation Procedure: The objective suggests that a term paper or unit paper would be an appropriate mode of evaluation to assess students' mastery of this objective. For complicated objectives of this nature it is often helpful if students are provided with the specific criteria that will be used to evaluate their responses. For example:

The following list of criteria will be used to assess your evaluation of the experimental study you select. In your response you should provide a discussion of the worth of the study selected with respect to the following items (you may include additional items if you wish):

A. Theoretical Worth
   1. To what extent was the problem researched a significant problem for investigation?
   2. To what extent did the researcher relate his/her specific problem of investigation to a theoretical basis?
   3. To what extent did the research contribute to the development or expansion of knowledge?
B. Methodological Worth
   1. To what extent were the operational definitions of the independent and dependent variables specified clearly?
   2. To what extent did the experimental design reflect the principles of internal and external validity?
   3. To what extent were appropriate statistical analyses applied to the data?

Affective Domain

1. Awareness

Objective: Given two weeks, the student will prepare a written "Journal of Interpersonal Communication," containing a description of the ways in which he/she increased sensitivity to others' problems and needs in at least five different types of communication situations.

Evaluation Procedure: The product to be evaluated is clear—i.e., the written "Journal of Interpersonal Communication." However, as with many objectives in the affective domain, the criteria for evaluation are not clearly specified. Specification of rigorous performance criteria for objectives of this nature often is not desirable because they place emphasis on the indicator(s) of goal achievement rather than on the goal itself (Wright and Doxsey, 1972). Even so, the evaluation procedure suggested here could provide the teacher with some index of student growth and development in terms of his/her interpersonal sensitivity, particularly if students were requested to prepare two "Journals of Interpersonal Communication"—one at the beginning of the term and one at the end. The teacher might then compare the two journals for each student on the basis of several possible criteria. For example, an increased sensitivity to others' problems and needs might be reflected in the nature of the communication events reported—e.g., from events involving communication with only close friends and relatives to events involving communication with mere acquaintances. Student learning might also be indexed by appropriate changes in the students' criteria for determining what is a communicative event that provides one with the opportunity to be sensitive to the needs and problems of others.

2. Valuing

Objective: Given one week, the student will observe several national and local news programs and write a five-page (minimum) paper in which the student's personal criteria are used to evaluate the worth of freedom (i.e., not censoring) in news reporting.

Evaluation Procedure: The evaluation procedure suggested in the objective is again in a written form. However, the objective could be modified to allow assessment of the student's ability to present his/her thoughts orally to classmates. The oral presentation may have an additional advantage in that it may generate discussion/disagreement among students and provide an index of students' ability to tolerate differing points of view.

3. Organization

Objective: Given an art object of his/her choice, the student will identify the characteristics of the art object he/she admires and construct a work of art that reflects these characteristics.

Evaluation Procedure: The mode of evaluation is clear (i.e., construction of an art object) and in this case differs from the oral or written modes. While flexibility and freedom for creativity would appear important in this objective, the evaluation procedure perhaps could be made more useful if students were required to specify the characteristics that the art object they construct is supposed to reflect. The teacher and classmates might then be in a position to provide useful feedback to the student regarding the extent to which the characteristics are clearly reflected in the art object.

Psychomotor Domain

1. Set

Objective: Given no prompting or reference materials, the student will demonstrate five basic ballet positions with a minimum rating of five by two of three judges (on a seven-point scale).

Evaluation Procedure: The use of rating scales for evaluation purposes requires the teacher to state clearly and concisely the specific criteria that will be used to assess students' performance. Once criteria are specified, it is a good idea to provide students with a copy of the rating scales so they know precisely what criteria will be used to judge their performance. Rating scales also allow the opportunity to employ peer-group evaluation, which provides students with practice in making judgments about others' performance using the same criteria that they are required to meet for their own performances.

2. Guided Responses

Objective: Given a demonstration on how to operate a wood lathe, the student will demonstrate the steps in operating a wood lathe following the recommended safety precautions outlined in the class handout.

Evaluation Procedure: While mastery of this objective could be assessed with a paper and pencil test, more complex psychomotor behaviors probably should be assessed under conditions that more closely approximate, or are exactly like, the actual behavior to be performed. Testing of this sort provides students with practice and also affords the opportunity for the teacher to supply immediate feedback.

3. Complex Overt Response

Objective: Given an unadjusted carburetor and one hour, the student will adjust the carburetor so it operates at maximum capacity.

Evaluation Procedure: The same comment applies here as in the preceding example.

While we have reduced the procedures in implementing a criterion-referenced evaluation system to only three steps, it should be clear that such implementation is seldom accomplished without some difficulties. The following sections are devoted to discussion of four of the most pervasive problems confronting the teacher using a criterion-referenced evaluation system.

IMPLEMENTATION OF A CRITERION-REFERENCED SYSTEM—
SELECTED PROBLEMS[1]

BRANCHING OPTION FOUR

The material contained in pages 128–133 is rather technical in nature. To obtain a firm understanding of the material, it is necessary for you to have a moderately sophisticated background in test construction, measurement theory, and statistics. However, we suggest that you read the material even if you now have some question about your ability to understand it fully. Perhaps your instructor will clarify any questions you may have. If you feel that you cannot understand the material, turn to page 133 and begin reading the section titled "Mastery Learning."

---

[1]Adapted from Mary-Jeanette Smythe, Robert J. Kibler, and Patricia W. Hutchings, "A Comparison of Norm-Referenced and Criterion-Referenced Measurement With Implications for Communication Instruction," *The Speech Teacher* 22, 1973, 1–17. Reprinted by permission of the authors and the Speech Communication Association.

Determination of Criterion for Mastery

The conceptual model of criterion-referenced measurement rests upon the premise that this method of evaluation will provide valid evidence regarding a student's learning of relevant skills or concepts. Complete operational definition of such mastery, therefore, depends upon the establishment of an absolute performance standard against which the adequacy of each student's learning may be weighed and judged. Such a standard should specify the exact proportion of the skills tested that a student must exhibit before he/she can be said to have mastered some particular content; it should be absolute in the sense that it is set prior to evaluation and serves as the sole criterion against which each student's performance is assessed. This inevitably raises the question of how the teacher selects the criterion values to be used. Although this is one question which is not yet satisfactorily resolved, and which is of sufficient complexity that it precludes discussion in this work of all the details involved in a criterion selection decision, some general observations seem to be warranted.

It may be useful to regard a criterion as a cutting score or a limiting value of a given proficiency range (Glaser and Nitko, 1971). Typically, these criteria are expressed by stating percent values, e.g., 80 percent, 90 percent, or 100 percent, or numbers, e.g., seven of ten, twenty of twenty-five, as the minimum acceptable level of mastery. Stated in this way, the criterion values may be used to denote both the quantity and the quality demands of the behavioral objective. What frequently occurs in practice when criteria are set is that the teacher initially makes an arbitrary decision based on his/her experience and subsequently modifies the criterion value over time as a function of the relative importance of the behaviors being evaluated. Performance norms from test administrations with previous samples of students may also provide a basis for decision. In the absence of any concrete information regarding student entering behavior, or the hierarchy of probable responses, raw intuition may be the only available guide to an initial selection of the criterion value. Reliance upon the intuitive powers of competent and experienced teachers working cooperatively is particularly helpful in setting standards. Until a systematic set of rules applicable to a broad spectrum of curricula is developed, the process of criterion selection will require teacher insight and judgment.

Observation of existing criterion-referenced measurement systems suggests at least two cautions with regard to criterion selection (Kriewall,

1972). First, adherence to a rigid criterion selection policy, without consideration of its consequences, is a dubious practice. A number of factors, including the nature of the tested material, frequency of testing, and test format characteristics, probably interact with the criterion value and affect student performance. Fixed criterion policies are viable only when sampling plans have been analyzed for each unit to ensure content validity of the criterion-referenced measurement and when considerable attention has been given to the decision implications inherent in the selection of the test length with the criterion value. Otherwise, the teacher may be compelled to use irrelevant test items to maintain uniform test lengths or, worse still, require students to attain a criterion that is optimum for longer tests, but unrealistically high on shorter tests.

Secondly, the mistaken belief that selecting a higher criterion value will result in a better quality of learning product should be abandoned. In almost all cases, this practice leads to a high probability of false negatives because the permissible margin for error is so narrow that the majority of tested students may fail to demonstrate mastery. Even the most carefully constructed criterion-referenced measurement, or norm-referenced measurement for that matter, is seldom a sufficiently stable or representative instrument to warrant a very high (90 or 100 percent) criterion value. Moreover, teachers must consider the affective, as well as the cognitive, consequences of performance standards. Assuming that students can be compelled to achieve consistently at the 90 or 95 percent level, are these cognitive outcomes meaningful enough to offset the possibility that the high performance standard makes instruction and evaluation procedures repugnant to students? The problem here is to find the admissible, if not optimum, solution that will maximize the positive development of learning, cognitively as well as affectively. Although further research to resolve this issue is indicated, available data suggest that setting the criterion for mastery at 85 percent may be optimal (Block, 1970).

Variability

The theory and method associated with the study of measurement in psychology and education has been developed in relation to psychological testing. The measurement concept of variability, the extent to which a group of scores tends to be homogeneous with regard to the specific trait being measured, has a decided influence on the interpretation of test scores. According to Popham and Husek (1969), the variability problem is the central theoretical and operational distinction between criterion-referenced measurement and norm-referenced measurement. On a theoretical level, variability determines the meaningfulness of norm-referenced measurement scores. The student is evaluated in terms of the position of his/her score in comparison with all other scores on the same norm-referenced measurement. Generally, the more variability in the scores on norm-referenced measurement, the better the test. Variability is largely ignored in assigning meaning to criterion-referenced measurement scores. The student is evaluated with regard to how closely his/her score approximates an established standard of performance. Consequently, the degree of variability obtained in criterion-referenced measurement scores is not necessarily related to the quality of the test.

Operationally, variability exercises a powerful effect on both norm-referenced and criterion-referenced approaches to testing. Traditional methods of test development and assessment, based on variability, are available for norm-referenced measurement. Criterion-referenced analogues to these methods of determining the reliability and validity of tests, however, have been slow to develop. As a result, the teacher who decides to implement criterion-referenced measurement must be prepared to discard certain measurement concepts as traditionally defined. A discussion of these concepts follows.

Item Analysis. Regardless of how painstakingly criterion-based tests are constructed, traditional methods of evaluating norm-referenced tests may be inappropriate for criterion-referenced measurement because these methods depend on variability of scores (Popham and Husek, 1969). Although one can argue that in practice the performance of students on criterion-referenced measurement may vary (Livingston, 1970), the possibility that scores on criterion-referenced measurement may have little or no variance does cast doubt on the relevance of the concept of reliability as defined within classical test theory. Still, efforts to ascertain the internal consistency of criterion-referenced measurement should not be abandoned prematurely.

In norm-referenced measurement, item analysis procedures are typically employed as a basis for rejecting items that do not properly discriminate among students taking the test. Since a criterion-referenced measurement is used to determine mastery or nonmastery of specified criterion behaviors rather than to differentiate individuals in a group, application of typical discrimination indices should be modified to accommodate the assumptions underlying criterion-referenced measurement. Cox and Vargas

(1966) have suggested an index based on the percentage of students who passed an item on a posttest minus the percentage of those who passed the same item on a pretest. Generating hypothetical frequencies based on the median value of each subtest, Popham (1970) has used chi-square to estimate the pre- and postinstructional relationship of individual test items. Hsu (1971) has developed an item discrimination index derived from the difference between the proportion of students who attain the criterion score on a test and answer a test item correctly and the proportion of students who do not achieve the criterion score and yet who still answer an item correctly. An item that has a larger proportion of correct responses in the group failing to achieve the criterion, then, discriminates negatively and should be reconsidered.

Regarding the omission of criterion-referenced measurement test items that appear to discriminate poorly or negatively between mastery and nonmastery groups, two considerations seem to be in order. First, non-discriminatory items are not necessarily inadequate items if they reflect an important aspect of the specified criterion behavior. If the item is indeed relevant to the performance objective, then the effectiveness of the intervening instruction may be at fault. Further, the item analyst should be sensitive to patterns in item discrimination. Should items measuring a certain class of behaviors be consistently poor or negative discriminators, then the specifications of the criterion must be questioned. In this sense, item analysis procedures may provide an empirical check on the validity of the construct that the criterion-referenced text was designed to measure (Jackson, 1970).

Reliability. An estimate of test reliability, the degree to which all items on a test are measuring the same behaviors is no less desirable for criterion-referenced measurement than for norm-referenced measurement. Unfortunately, the troublesome issue of score variability, upon which classical reliability procedures are based, restricts the options available to the criterion-based test constructor. Compounding the problem is the absence of any alternative procedures that are data based and of demonstrated empirical validity. On the basis of a modification of classical reliability theory, Livingston (1972) has proposed a criterion-referenced measurement reliability coefficient that is derived by substituting the criterion score of a test for the mean test score in the formula for computing the coefficient. Although the procedure has been challenged by Harris (1972), Hsu (1971) cites some data demonstrating that the results obtained from Livingston's formula are roughly comparable to those obtained from the Kuder-Richardson 20 formula. [Note: The K-R 20 formula is only one of several definitions of internal consistency.]

A somewhat different approach, involving independently developed parallel forms of a criterion-based test, would estimate reliability through an index of agreement between the scores obtained on the two tests. In discussing this method, Jackson (1970) suggests categorizing scores according to some nominal classification and then computing a contingency coefficient to obtain a reliability estimate.

Assuming that a measure of reliability is achieved, are there methods to refine the criterion-referenced test so that it will be a more precise and stable instrument? In norm-referenced measurement the time-honored strategies are to delete ambiguous items, develop standard and clear instructions, and add more items of equal quality and kind. Completion of these operations will, likewise, facilitate the development of better criterion-referenced measurement. When the behaviors specified in the criterion are complex, the need for extra items to sample the domain adequately is particularly acute. Similarly, ambiguities in objectives, instructions, or test items are never desirable.

Perhaps the single most effective method of ensuring precision and accuracy in criterion-referenced measurement, though, is the careful matching of test items to performance objectives. When the behaviors are clearly delineated for student and teacher alike and a systematic testing plan is implemented, objectivity and accuracy should be among the consequences.

MASTERY LEARNING

An additional concept relating to evaluation, which is particularly suited to a criterion-referenced system and which is consistent with the philosophy of the general model of instruction presented in this book, is the concept of *mastery learning*. Simply stated, mastery learning proposes that all, or almost all, students can master given instructional objectives at high standards of performance. While effective mastery-learning strategies have been developed only recently (Bloom, Hastings, and Madaus, 1971), the concept of mastery learning is not entirely new (Washburne, 1922; Morrison, 1926). However, the recent interest in and development of effective mastery-learning strategies received impetus from Carroll's (1963) model of foreign language learning. Carroll found that students' ability to learn language predicted not only the level of competency they attained in a given time period, but also the amount of time students required to attain a given level of competency. Consequently, rather than viewing student aptitudes as an index of the level of learning that could be attained, Carroll defined aptitudes as an index of the amount of time students required to master a given criterion level under ideal instructional conditions (Block, 1971). In effect, Carroll's model proposed that if a student were allowed the time needed to master given subject matter content and if he/she spent the required time in appropriate instructional activities, then it could be expected that the student would attain mastery of the subject matter.

In a later article dealing with the concept of mastery learning, Bloom (1968) argued that if students were distributed normally with respect to aptitude for a given subject and if they received the same instruction (i.e., in terms of quality and time), then student achievement would also be normally distributed (Block, 1971).[2] Bloom's argument in effect describes the traditional, norm-referenced type of evaluation system that characterizes most current educational systems. The relationship between aptitude and achievement in the traditional, norm-referenced evaluation system is represented in Figure 5.

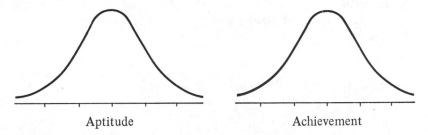

Aptitude   Achievement

FIGURE 5. The Relationship Between Aptitude and Achievement in the Traditional Norm-Referenced System

Following Carroll's (1963) model, Bloom (1968) further argued that if students were distributed normally with respect to aptitude but received quality instruction and were allowed needed time to master content, then

[2]Most research on aptitude and achievement suggests only a 30 to 40 percent correspondence rather than a one-to-one correspondence. Also, it should be noted that, technically, random error is the only thing that is distributed normally, not psychological traits, as indicated in the curves in Figures 5 and 6. The curves are depicted as they are for illustrative purposes.

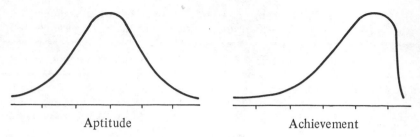

Aptitude   Achievement

*FIGURE 6.   The Relationship Between Aptitude and Achievement
in the Mastery-Learning System*

one could expect little or no relationship between aptitude and achievement. The relationship between aptitude and achievement in the mastery-learning system is represented in Figure 6.[3]

The key aspect of the mastery-learning system is that it allows each student to spend whatever time is needed to master content before he/she is presented with new material. Consequently, in the pure mastery-learning system students are allowed unlimited opportunities to demonstrate mastery of instructional objectives. As such, application of a pure mastery-learning system is obviously not practical for most current educational systems. However, there are alternatives to a pure mastery system. One alternative is what we shall refer to as a modified mastery-learning system, which is examined in the following section.

Table 3 (pp. 136–137) is designed to illustrate and summarize the fundamental differences between a traditional and a mastery-learning system. While some of the contrasts presented in Table 3 may appear overgeneralized, they have been so designed to stress the extremes inherent in the two systems.

Modified Mastery Learning

As already indicated, implementation of a pure mastery-learning system is in most instances impractical within the currently established

---

[3]Note that achievement in a pure mastery-learning system is more appropriately depicted as a bi-modal curve indicating mastery or nonmastery of objectives. However, in a modified mastery-learning system where student performance is translated into a standard grading format (i.e., A,B,C,D,F), achievement is more appropriately depicted as it is in Figure 6. The next section will examine grading procedures with a modified mastery-learning system.

*TABLE 3. Contrasts of Selected Characteristic Assumptions
of the Traditional Education Systems and Mastery Learning*

Traditional System	Mastery-Learning System
1. Students entering a course/school year have approximately the same competencies.	1. Students have varied entering behaviors (competencies) at the beginning of instruction for a course/school year.
2. For efficiency, students are grouped into three basic learning levels, i.e., superior, average, and slow learners.	2. Students are not grouped but are assessed on an individual basis.
3. Course planning is usually oriented toward the material to be covered.	3. Course planning is oriented toward desired terminal performances.
4. The teacher's role is primarily that of an information-dispenser.	4. The teacher's role is primarily that of a learning manager, e.g., selecting and developing appropriate instructional strategies based on individual students' needs to achieve objectives.
5. A given instructional strategy is selected and designed to be most effective and efficient for most students.	5. Instructional strategies are selected and designed for individual competencies and learning styles.
6. Generally, instruction focuses on the "average" student.	6. Instruction focuses on the individual student.
7. Responsibility for achievement rests primarily with the student.	7. Responsibility for student achievement is primarily the teacher's (or is shared with student).
8. Students achieve in a normally distributed manner that is reflected in their performance.	8. Students achieve at or below a given level of mastery (previously specified criterion) that is reflected in their performance.
9. A student's performance is often evaluated by comparing *him/her* with other students.	9. A student's performance is evaluated by comparing *it* with an absolute standard (prespecified criterion).

TABLE 3. (Continued)

Traditional System	Mastery-Learning System
10. Periodic assessments (e.g., midterms, unit tests, quizzes) are for determining the current levels of achievement, and the student almost always continues *regardless* of his/her performance.	10. Formative (periodic) evaluations are for diagnostic purposes and are independent of the summative (final) evaluation, the result of which is to recycle students' learning or permit them to progress.
11. Periodic evaluations and/or final exams are used to determine a final grade, usually by some averaging procedure.	11. Summative evaluations are for grading (i.e., determining if criterion has been achieved) such as pass-fail or S-U procedure.
12. The necessity for recycling (repeating) is determined only at the conclusion of the course/ school year.	12. Recycling is necessary at any stage of the instruction at which criterion is not met.
13. Students leaving a course/school year have a wide range of competencies in achieving the general objectives.	13. Most (ideally, all) students achieve a previously established, criterion level of mastery before beginning the next segment of instruction.
14. Teachers are not accountable for student learning.	14. Teachers are accountable for how well students learn.

From G. Robert Spell, Robert J. Kibler, and Arlie Muller Parks, "A Comparison of Mastery and Traditional Learning Systems with Selected Implications for Speech Communication Instruction." Paper presented at the meeting of the International Communication Association, Atlanta, Georgia, April 1972. Reprinted by permission of the authors.

educational systems. An alternative to a pure mastery-learning system is what we prefer to call a modified mastery-learning system. The modified system differs from the pure system in two ways that are important to concerns about practicality regarding implementation. The modified mastery-learning system places a limit on (1) the amount of time given to students to demonstrate mastery of instructional objectives and (2) the number of opportunities students have for demonstrating mastery of instructional objectives.

Regarding the limitation of time, students in a modified mastery-learning system are required to master instructional objectives for an entire

.course within the specified time limit determined by the educational system (e.g., a semester, a quarter, a year, etc.). The specific working procedures for implementing the system usually can be left to the teacher's discretion. For example, a teacher may require students to master objectives for a given unit of instruction within a specified time limit (e.g., two weeks, three weeks, etc.), or the teacher may allow students to recycle through units at their own pace as long as they complete all units of the course within a specified period of time. Decisions about specific working procedures depend upon such matters as the nature of the subject matter (e.g., sequentially dependent or independent units), the availability of individualized instructional materials (e.g., programed texts, reading materials), student preferences, and limitations on the teacher for spending time with students who need additional instruction. Usually a teacher can find some means for implementing a workable system within the particular limitations of time and facilities of his/her educational institution.

The second aspect of the modified mastery-learning system can be implemented by using multiple test forms for each unit of evaluation in the course. The number of test forms employed would then serve to define the number of chances students have to improve performance on a particular unit of instruction. For example, if a course consisted of three units, a teacher might develop four forms of each unit test (e.g., a total of twelve tests). For each unit of the course students would then be given a maximum of four chances to improve mastery of the objectives. It is difficult to offer a general statement about how many test forms a teacher should use. The decision would be determined, in part, by limitations of time and the nature of the subject matter. However, we suggest beginning with two forms at least of each test. Examining the results of student performance across a few quarters (terms, years, or whatever) would determine if two forms of each test appear to provide enough opportunity for most students to succeed in the course at a fairly high level. If this turns out to be the case (our experience indicates that it usually is), there is no need to develop additional test forms. However, if examination of student performance suggests that the majority of students need additional opportunities to demonstrate mastery, then developing and employing additional test forms should be considered.

Grading in a Modified Mastery-Learning System

When an educational institution employs a dichotomous grading system, such as pass-fail or satisfactory-unsatisfactory, as an index of student achievement, there is little or no problem in implementing a modified mastery-learning system. However, in most instances educational institutions use a graduated index of student achievement (e.g., A, B, C, D, F). When a graduated index is used, the teacher must be able to translate student performance within the mastery-learning system into the type of grading procedure used by his/her school system. A way of making this translation is to set criterion levels for minimum acceptable performance that correspond to the grading scale of the educational institution. One method for achieving the correspondence is for the teacher to require that a prespecified minimum number—or percentage—of instructional objectives be mastered for each particular grade level. For example, the teacher might require students to master 90 to 100 percent of the objectives for a given unit of instruction in order to receive an A, while mastery of 80 to 89 percent of the objectives would be required to attain a B, and so on. While this strategy can be used to translate grades from a mastery system to a traditional one, there is at least one problem in using this particular method. The method implies that all (or most) of the objectives for a given unit of instruction are of equal value in terms of complexity and/or importance. In other words, this method makes it possible for a student to obtain an A, for example, for a given unit of instruction even though he/she failed to demonstrate mastery of some of the most important objectives for the unit. An alternative to this method is to classify the objectives for a given unit of instruction into separate categories based on their importance, value, and/or complexity. The teacher then might specify minimum criterion levels for mastery of objectives within each category. For example, students might be required to master all of the objectives in one category and only 90 percent of the objectives in another category in order to receive an A for a given unit of instruction. This method also has drawbacks, since it may require the teacher to keep rather complicated progress reports on each student to determine which category of objectives the student has mastered and which he/she has not. The method also might entail an exorbitant amount of paper work for the teacher during retesting with alternative forms to insure that each student is being retested over the appropriate category or categories of objectives. A third alternative, and by far one of the easiest, is to include a representative sample (in terms of importance and/or complexity) of objectives on each test over a given unit of instruction. The sample of objectives for inclusion on the test should be such that a high level of performance cannot be attained on the test unless a reasonable number of important/complex objectives have been mastered. If this condition is met, then mastery of a minimum number or percentage of objectives for each grade level may be specified without the potential problems of the first alternative.

A final note should be made about grading in a modified mastery-learning system. The teacher should avoid using a grading procedure that relies on a cumulative point system or averaging of grades across instructional units to determine students' final grades for a course. Such procedures make it possible for students to obtain a moderate to low (e.g., B to D) level of mastery for one or more units of instruction and still obtain a high level of mastery (e.g., an A) for the entire course. While this may not appear problematic on the surface, it does in effect negate the logic of a criterion-referenced, mastery-learning evaluation system. Ideally, a grade of A in a mastery-learning system indicates that a student has mastered the objectives across all units of a course at an A level. However, since we are concerned with implementation of a modified mastery-learning system, wherein limits are set on the amount of time and test opportunities students have to demonstrate mastery, the teacher may consider such ideal standards too stringent to be implemented practically. If this is the case, the teacher may devise a set of rules for determining final course grades that allow for more flexibility (i.e., room for student error). Incidentally, it probably is a good idea to build some flexibility of this nature into the grading system to account for possible measurement error. An example of a flexible grading system might be one following rules similar to these for a four unit course:

To obtain an A in the course, you must:

1. obtain an A on each unit test (first *or* second form) plus an A on the outside project;

OR

2. obtain a total of three A's on unit tests and/or the outside project and *only one B.*

To obtain a B in the course, you must:

1. obtain at least a B on each unit test (first *or* second form) and at least a B on the outside project;

OR

2. obtain a total of at least three B's on unit tests and/or the outside project and *only one C.*

To obtain a C in the course, you must:

1. obtain at least a C on unit tests (first *or* second form) and at least a C on the outside project;

OR

2. obtain a total of at least three C's on unit tests and/or the outside project and *only one D.*

To obtain a D in the course, you must:

1. obtain at least a D on each unit test (first *or* second form) and at least a D on the outside project;

OR

2. obtain a total of at least three D's on unit tests and/or the outside project and *only one F.*

To obtain a F in the course, you may:

1. fail to take either form of the unit tests and/or fail to complete the outside project;

OR

2. perform below the minimum requirement for a D on *two* or more unit tests or one unit test *and* the outside project.

SUMMARY

This chapter focused on the fourth component of the general model of instruction. Our discussion of evaluation procedures in the model hinged on two concepts: criterion-referenced evaluation and mastery learning. Criterion-referenced evaluation was defined and distinguished from the traditional norm-referenced evaluation system. The procedures for implementing a criterion-referenced evaluation system were outlined. These

142 Evaluation

procedures included: (1) the specification of instructional objectives, (2) the selection of appropriate evaluation procedures to assess students' mastery of stated objectives, and (3) the matching of particular evaluation procedures with performance behaviors specified in objectives. The section on criterion-referenced evaluation ended with an examination of selected problems in implementing a criterion-referenced system.

The section on mastery learning described the work of Carroll (1963) and Bloom (1968) in formulating the basic logic of a mastery-learning system. It was suggested that implementation of a pure mastery-learning system is in most instances impractical. Consequently, the procedures for implementing a modified mastery-learning system were presented. The modified system differs from the pure system in two ways that are important regarding the practicality of implementing the system. The modified mastery-learning system places a limit on (1) the amount of time given to students to demonstrate mastery of instructional objectives and (2) the number of opportunities students have for demonstrating mastery of instructional objectives. The chapter concluded with an examination of various procedures for translating student performance within a modified mastery-learning system into a graduated grade index.

7

THE INFLUENCE OF INSTRUCTIONAL OBJECTIVES IN EDUCATION

After completing this chapter, the learner should be able to:

1. Describe the relationship between the educational level of learners (i.e., elementary, secondary, and higher education) and the difficulty in specifying/measuring instructional objectives;
2. Identify at least three values that instructional objectives have for students;
3. Identify at least two values that instructional objectives have for teachers;
4. Describe how instructional objectives can aid administrators;
5. Describe how instructional objectives can aid educators in communicating with school boards and parents.

The first section of this chapter covers the implications of using instructional objectives at various educational grade levels. The second section discusses how these objectives may be used by various participants involved in the educational process. The third section examines the influence of the school environment on the objectives.

APPLICATION OF INSTRUCTIONAL OBJECTIVES TO SPECIFIED EDUCATIONAL LEVELS

Discussions in previous chapters may have given some readers the impression that an instructional objective for one educational level is not much different from an objective for another educational level. It is time to clear up any such misconceptions.

Personal experience and developmental research suggest that individuals acquire capacities to perform different skills and intellectual operations at various periods during development (Bloom, 1964; McDonald, 1965; McCandless, 1967; DeCecco, 1968). Behavior patterns for a given individual vary in rate of development and may vary substantially from individual to individual (Edwards and Scannell, 1968). Moreover, students of learning also may recall that there are a variety of types of learning, that these different types of learning may be sequential, and that a given type of learning may be contingent upon previously learned behaviors (Glaser, 1962; Gagné, 1965a and 1965b).

Obviously, the extent and kind of information to be acquired, applied, analyzed, synthesized, and evaluated differ between preschool and graduate programs. The specific psychomotor skills and attitudes to be acquired also vary as a function of educational level.

Instructional objectives must be viewed in light of many different variables in the educational setting. Perhaps one of the more critical variables that affects their use is the level of education for which objectives are intended. Several important distinctions among objectives at differing educational levels should be pointed out.

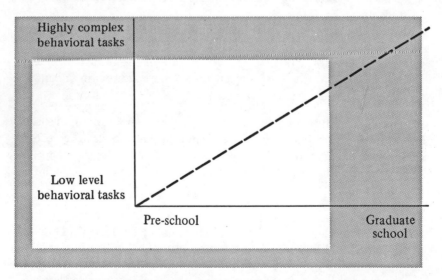

FIGURE 7. Generalized Relationship Speculated Between Grade Levels and Complexity of Tasks Required

Figure 7 emphasizes a *general tendency:* as the educational level increases, the complexity of behaviors (and objectives) required increases. But the relationship suggested in Figure 7 is just a tendency. We do not intend to imply a one-to-one relationship regarding educational level and task complexity. Anyone who has taught in an elementary classroom knows that small children are capable of performing some very complex tasks. However, the child in the first grade most likely will be given objectives that emphasize the acquisition of basic skills frequently implemented through drill and practice, while students in higher education situations frequently will be given objectives that emphasize applying, organizing, problem solving, and other concept manipulation tasks. The point is, it frequently becomes more difficult to formulate objectives and measure the outcomes of instruction as the educational level increases.

The relationship between grade level and observable behaviors is exceedingly complex and cannot be expressed completely in a simple graph. It is possible to express a *general tendency* for the two to be related, and we have done this in Figure 8. Again, a *tendency* is being expressed in Figure 8; there is no intention to imply a one-to-one relationship. Figure 8 emphasizes that the behaviors desired at lower educational levels frequently are observable (e.g., psychomotor behaviors), while behaviors

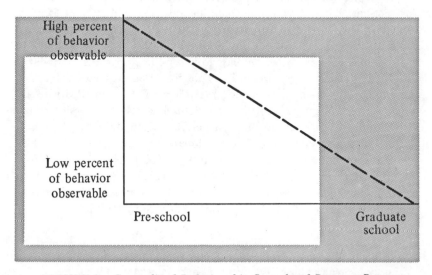

FIGURE 8. Generalized Relationship Speculated Between Percent of Behavior Observable and Grade Levels

desired at higher levels tend to be less observable (often affective and cognitive behaviors).[1] An objective for a child of kindergarten age, such as "place the square block in the square hole," involves considerably less complex skills than an objective for a postdoctoral seminar, such as "given the desired characteristics of a proposed synthetic plastic, develop a material that meets the desired specifications and provide a projected cost analysis for full-scale production."

It follows from the above contentions that the learner increases (or should increase) his/her responsibility for learning quite rapidly as educational levels increase. Increasing the complexity and decreasing the observable behaviors as a function of educational level suggest the learner has little option but to become a more independent learner.

The higher the level of instruction, the more ambiguous and difficult to measure are the objectives. Many objectives at higher levels involve learning outside the context of the classroom. The result is that the observable behaviors are reduced for product evaluation. At lower levels most learning of desired skills occurs in class under the observation of the teacher. The measurement of these skills is made easier and more complete. Ideally, as the level of education increases, the relationship between instructional objectives and competencies required for real-life tasks also increases.

Realizing that such differences occur when using objectives at different instructional levels, teachers and administrators should attempt to adapt the specificity level and measurement level of objectives to appropriate grade levels or, better still, to the levels of individual students. Moreover, instructional objectives that are based on real-life competencies should be specified as soon and as frequently as possible. Measurement of objectives should be attempted at all levels, regardless of the complexity of the objective or the ambiguity of the task desired. Successful measurement is dependent not only on level of instruction but on the creativity of the instructional planner and objective developer.

Some of the early work of Bobbitt (1918, 1924), Charters (1923, 1928), and Charters and Waples (1929), in which systematic procedures were employed to formulate detailed objectives for education, provides some indication of the complexity gradient at various grade levels.

---

[1]This observation was first suggested to one of the authors by William R. McKenzie of Southern Illinois University in a doctoral seminar in 1966.

THE RELATIONSHIP OF INSTRUCTIONAL OBJECTIVES TO PARTICIPANTS IN THE EDUCATIONAL PROCESS

The philosophy underlying the use of instructional objectives has already been discussed in a previous chapter. The purpose of this section is to illustrate how the philosophy applies to those persons directly or indirectly involved with the educational process. Instructional objectives serve all who are involved in the teaching-learning process, particularly students, teachers, administrators, school boards, and parents (Kibler and Barker, 1970).

Instructional Objectives and Students

Research concerned with the transfer of learning indicates that students generally do not apply learned skills or knowledge to practical situations unless the teacher specifically demonstrates the application. The popular phrase in academic circles that reflects this body of research is "teach for transfer." The teacher attempting to implement this strategy makes desired behaviors explicit and specifies the variety of conditions under which the behaviors or skills may be applied after they have been adequately learned. When instructional objectives are given directly to students, the exact behaviors desired and the conditions under which the behaviors are to be exhibited are specified. By being given instructional objectives, students do not have to guess what is expected of them in the learning setting. Learners may spend their time acquiring behaviors specified by the teacher rather than attempting to infer what the teacher expects of them. It stands to reason that if students know what is expected of them, they will expend less random energy studying unimportant material and will concentrate on learning important skills.

One final value of giving instructional objectives to students is intangible yet very important. It is the sense of security a student experiences when he/she knows what specifically is expected from him/her in a course and the conditions under which he/she will be expected to exhibit competencies. Psychologists suggest that generalized fears cause greater emotional anxiety than specific, well-defined fears. Instructional objectives can help students understand specific requirements of a course and also reduce the amount of generalized anxiety about course requirements.

Instructional Objectives and Teachers[2]

The value of instructional objectives to the teacher is dependent, of course, upon the level of instruction, the subject matter of the course, the nature of the school system, and countless other variables related to the instructional environment. However, there appear to be at least two values of objectives (for teachers) that remain constant in most teaching situations. First, objectives prompt teachers to determine the most significant aspect of the subject matter to be learned. At the college level, students often joke that a specific course (e.g., Advanced Theories of Learning) is, in reality, a course in Professor X. In other words, the professor makes no attempt to define critical elements of subject matter related to the course but only talks about theories of learning of interest to him/her. In rare situations a course in Professor X may be desirable and useful, but from a curriculum viewpoint such a course creates a void of information in a student's educational background that might be important in the future. If teachers discipline themselves to analyze the content of specific courses for which they are responsible, the problem of majoring on minors or dwelling on unimportant issues will become less critical. It should be emphasized at this point that this value of objectives is not held universally by all educators.

A second value of objectives to teachers is their aid in establishing criteria for the measurement of classroom achievement. Most teachers have had the experience of teaching a unit in a course and then spending long, torturous hours attempting to devise ways of measuring what the students have learned. Teachers often find that had they approached the subject matter in a slightly different manner or modified instructional strategies, the measure of classroom achievement could have been greatly simplified and improved (i.e., made more reliable and valid). Instructional objectives require teachers to specify criteria for acceptable behaviors and determine in advance how acceptable performance will be measured. Thus measurement in the classroom may be improved.

A side effect of these two values for teachers is similar to that experienced by students. The teacher who is confident (1) that the subject matter being presented is of prime importance and (2) that measurement

---

[2]Teachers interested in an opportunity to share their behavioral objectives with other teachers and to obtain copies of objectives used by other teachers will want to read Appendix D, which briefly explains a program to encourage the exchange of behavioral objectives.

of achievement is efficient and appropriate to course goals is more secure in his/her position and, consequently, is usually more satisfied with his/her professional contribution.

Instructional Objectives and Administrators

Instructional objectives are important at two levels of administration. The administrator responsible for designing and coordinating curricula (in conjunction with the instructional staff) relies on instructional objectives to insure that content and subject matter are covered adequately and that there are minimal overlaps between courses, especially within related areas. The use of instructional objectives also promotes consistency and a thread of continuity among related courses. Continuity is especially important in a series of courses where there is an introductory section followed by an intermediate or advanced section.

When the administrator is supervisor and teacher-evaluator, instructional objectives help him/her in a different way. The objectives (1) suggest the degree of progress desired at a point in the course in light of the predetermined sequence of units and (2) help determine whether teachers are pursuing adequately the goals of the course. When the instructional objectives are developed by the teacher, they give the supervising administrator insight into the teacher's philosophy and course goals. This freedom to develop individual objectives is more prevalent at higher levels of instruction.

Instructional Objectives and School Boards

One of the persistent problems in education is to obtain adequate funds for the maintenance of a quality educational program. *School board* refers to the group of citizens who control funds in an educational setting. In the college context the term *board of trustees* or perhaps the *committee on education* would be substituted for the term *school board*.

In order to defend an existing budget or demonstrate the need for increased funds, administrators and teachers often are required to describe the existing educational program or some proposed addition to the curriculum. It is difficult to provide the board with a verbal or verbal-pictorial representation of the learning situation as it really exists because board members are often far removed from the classroom. However, when a school system requires instructional objectives for courses, it is possible to demonstrate the content of courses in objective form to a school board and thus demonstrate, more concretely than might otherwise be possible, precisely what learning achievements occur in a given classroom on a given day. This concrete representation of the educational program often may have some communicative or persuasive value to a school board. Thus, instructional objectives may help educate and persuade those persons in charge of educational funds.

Instructional Objectives and Parents

The parent is often neglected as a participant in the educational process. However, parents are becoming increasingly concerned about the quality of education in the school and are, therefore, becoming more involved with their children's educational growth and classroom problems. When students are given instructional objectives, the parents may also elect to study them and determine what behaviors are expected of their child during the school year. Although we are unaware of the existence of such a practice, we feel that a procedure of periodically sending home a list of the actual objectives achieved by a student would be a marked improvement over the grade report-card procedure commonly used. Parents could thereby gauge the progress of their child at intervals during the year to help insure that proper levels of achievement are being maintained. It is, of course, desirable that parents confer with teachers as well as with their children about educational achievement, but the presence of instructional objectives can serve to make parents more familiar with the child's desired growth and, in some instances, indicate areas where the child needs special help outside of the classroom.

Parents may be overly concerned about minor points in the curriculum that were stressed when they were in school. The specification of *major* objectives can help parents emphasize and reinforce the goals being sought by the teacher and can alleviate tendencies on the part of some parents to stress relatively unimportant concepts to their children.

THE ENVIRONMENT OF THE SCHOOL AND THE USE OF INSTRUCTIONAL OBJECTIVES

The educational environment in a classroom or within departments of a university can influence profoundly the value and use of instructional objectives. In the homogeneous classroom or in the college class primarily composed of majors in a given discipline, the objectives will probably be more valuable and realistic in light of the criteria specified for measuring desired achievement. When heterogeneous classes exist and when college courses include students with a variety of interests and major areas of study, the specification of performance criteria is often unrealistic for students at extreme ends of the achievement continuum. Therefore, the objectives should be flexible when possible and primarily serve as a guide rather than as a straight-jacket for the teacher. The teacher should analyze the socioeconomic and educational structure of students in a class and determine whether or not a set of rigid instructional objectives would be desirable and useful. This reemphasizes a point that was made earlier—that objectives must be tailored to individual needs. A set of blanket objectives could do more harm than good in some classes or types of educational programs.

A second environmental variable that relates to the success of the instructional objective is the attitude of the school system toward educational innovations. In a school system that encourages creative education, the objectives can serve to standardize content matter across modes of instruction, insuring that subject matter is not omitted or distorted as a result of the new teaching strategy. Instructional objectives appear to be more valuable in an educational environment where creativity and innovation is encouraged. Instructional objectives are also useful in an educational system that is static, but their value there is in curriculum standardization rather than in maintaining consistency across a wide variety of instructional strategies.

A school system's standards also affect the use of instructional objectives. When academic standards are emphasized and measured, objectives can provide assessments of educational progress and eliminate much subjectivity and guesswork in evaluation of teachers' and students' performance. In systems that have relaxed standards and do not attempt to evaluate teachers or students, objectives have less value.

In conclusion, the educational environment plays an important role in determining whether objectives can be profitable, desirable, and useful. Objectives must be geared to a given teacher and class in the context of a particular school system in order to be of maximum value.

REFERENCES

Airasian, P. W. The role of evaluation in mastery learning. In J. Block (Ed.), *Mastery learning: theory and practice.* New York: Holt, Rinehart and Winston, 1971.

Airasian, P. W., & Madaus, G. F. Criterion-referenced testing in the classroom. *The National Council on Measurement in Education (NCME)* 3 (4), 1972, 1–8.

Allen, D. W., & McDonald, F. J. The effects of self-instruction on learning in programmed instruction. Paper presented at the meeting of the American Educational Research Association, Chicago, Illinois, 1963.

Ammerman, H. L., & Melching, W. H. *The derivation, analysis, and classification of instructional objectives.* Alexandria: George Washington University, 1966.

Ammons, R. Effects of knowledge of performance: a survey and a tentative theoretical formulation. *Journal of General Psychology* 54, 1956, 279–299.

Andersen, K., & Clevenger, T. A summary of experimental research in ethos. *Speech Monographs* 30, 1963, 59–78.

Baker, E. L. Effects on student achievement of behavioral and nonbehavioral objectives. *The Journal of Experimental Education* 37, 1969, 5–8.

Bassett, R. E. The effects of student training in the use of behavioral objectives, and knowledge of test performance on learner achievement in a modified mastery learning course in speech communication. Unpublished doctoral dissertation, Florida State University, 1973.

Bishop, D. D. Effectiveness of prior exposure to performance objectives as a technique for improvement of student recall and retention. Unpublished doctoral dissertation, Ohio State University, 1969.

Blaney, J. P., & McKie, D. Knowledge of conference objectives and effect upon learning. *Adult Education Journal* 19, 1969, 98–105.

Block, J. H. The effects of various levels of performance on selected cognitive, affective and time variables. Unpublished doctoral dissertation, University of Chicago, 1970.

Block, J. H. Introduction to mastery learning: theory and practice. In J. H. Block (Ed.), *Mastery learning: theory and practice.* New York: Holt, Rinehart and Winston, Inc., 1971.

Bloom, B. S. *Stability and change in human characteristics.* New York: John Wiley & Sons, 1964.

Bloom, B. S. Learning for mastery. *Evaluation Comment* 1, 1968.

Bloom, B. S. (Ed.), Engelhart, N. D., Furst, E. J., Hill, W. H., & Krathwohl, D. R. *Taxonomy of educational objectives–the classification of educational goals, Handbook I: cognitive domain.* New York: David McKay Company, Inc., 1956.

Bloom, B. S., Hastings, J. T., & Madaus, G. F. *Handbook on formative and summative evaluation of student learning.* New York: McGraw-Hill, 1971.

Boardman, D. E. The effect of student's advanced knowledge of behavioral objectives on their achievement in remedial chemistry. Unpublished doctoral dissertation, University of California at Los Angeles, 1970.

Bobbitt, F. *The curriculum.* Boston: Houghton Mifflin, 1918.

Bobbitt, F. *How to make a curriculum.* Boston: Houghton Mifflin, 1924.

Briggs, L. J. *Sequencing of instruction in relation to hierarchies of competence.* Pittsburg, Pennsylvania: American Institutes for Research, 1968.

Brown, J. L. The effects of revealing instructional objectives on the learning of political concepts and attitudes in two role-playing games. Unpublished doctoral dissertation, University of California at Los Angeles, 1970.

Bryant, N. The effects of performance objectives on the achievement level of selected eighth-grade science pupils in four predominantly black inner-city schools. Unpublished doctoral dissertation, Indiana University, 1970.

Cardarelli, A. F. An investigation of the effect on pupil achievement when teachers are assigned and trained in the use of behavioral objectives. Unpublished doctoral dissertation, Syracuse University, 1971.

Carroll, J. A model of school learning. *Teachers College Record* 64, 1963, 723–733.

Cegala, D. J., Kibler, R. J., Barker, L. L., & Miles, D. T. Writing behavioral objectives: a programed article. *The Speech Teacher* 21, 1972, 151–168.

Charters, W. W. *Curriculum construction.* New York: Macmillan, 1923.

Charters, W. W. *The teaching of ideals.* New York: Macmillan, 1928.

Charters, W. W., & Waples, D. *The commonwealth teacher-training study.* Chicago: University of Chicago Press, 1929.

Chenzoff, A. P., & Folley, J. D., Jr. *Guidelines for training situation and analysis.* Technical report NAVTRADEVCEN 1218–4, Contract Number N 61339–1218. Valencia, Pennsylvania: Applied Science Associates, Inc., 1965.

Clingman, E. E. The impact of teacher and student knowledge of educational objectives on student learning and satisfaction. Unpublished doctoral dissertation, University of Wisconsin, 1972.

Commission on the Reorganization of Secondary Education. *Cardinal principles of secondary education.* Bulletin No. 35. Washington, D.C.: United States Government Printing Office, 1918.

Conlon, B. A. A comparison of the performance of seventh grade students with and without prior knowledge of the objectives of an individualized science program. Unpublished doctoral dissertation, Florida State University, 1970.

Cox, R. C., & Vargas, J. S. A comparison of item selection techniques for norm-referenced and criterion-referenced tests. Symposium presented at the meeting of the American Educational Research Association and the National Council on Measurement in Education, Chicago, February 1966.

Crooks, F. C. The differential effects of pre-prepared and teacher-prepared instructional objectives on the learning of educable mentally retarded children. Unpublished doctoral dissertation, University of Iowa, 1971.

Culbertson, F. Modification of an emotionally held attitude through role-playing. *Journal of Abnormal and Social Psychology* 54, 1957, 230–233.

Dalis, G. T. Effect of precise objectives upon student achievement in health education. *Journal of Experimental Education* 39, 1970, 20–23.

DeCecco, J. P. *The psychology of learning and instruction: educational psychology.* Englewood Cliffs, New Jersey: Prentice-Hall, 1968.

Doty, C. R. The effect of practice and prior knowledge of educational objectives on performance. Unpublished doctoral dissertation, Ohio State University, 1968.

Duchastel, P. C., & Merrill, P. F. The effects of behavioral objectives on learning: a review of empirical studies. *Review of Educational Research*, 43, 1973, 53–70.

Ebel, R. L. Behavioral objectives: a close look. *Phi Delta Kappan* 52, 1970, 171–173.

Educational Policies Commission. *The central purpose of American education.* Washington, D. C.: National Education Association, 1961.

Edwards, A. J., & Scannell, D. P. *Educational psychology: the teaching-learning process.* Scranton, Pennsylvania: International Textbook, 1968.

Eisner, E. W. Educational objectives: help or hindrance? *School Review* 75, 1967, 250–260.

Elam, S. The age of accountability dawns in Texarkana. *Phi Delta Kappan* 51, 1970, 509–515.

Engel, R. S. An experimental study of the effect of stated behavioral objectives on achievement in a unit of instruction on negative and rational base systems of numeration. Unpublished Master's thesis, University of Maryland, 1968.

English, H. B., & English, A. C. *A comprehensive dictionary of psychological and psychoanalytical terms.* New York: David McKay, 1958.

Ferre, A. V. Effects of repeated performance objectives upon student achievement and attitude. Unpublished doctoral dissertation, New Mexico State University, 1972.

French, W., & Associates. *Behavioral goals of general education in high school.* New York: Russell Sage Foundation, 1957.

Gagné, R. M. Educational objectives and human performances. In J. D. Krumboltz (Ed.), *Learning and the educational process.* Chicago: Rand McNally, 1965a.

Gagné, R. M. The analysis of instructional objectives for the design of instruction. In R. Glaser (Ed.), *Teaching machines and programed learning, II.* Washington, D.C.: National Education Association of the U.S., 1965b.

Gagné, R. M. *The conditions of learning.* 1st ed. New York: Holt, Rinehart and Winston, 1965c.

Gagné, R. M. *The conditions of learning.* 2nd ed. New York: Holt, Rinehart and Winston, 1970.

Geis, G. L. *Behavioral objectives: a selected bibliography and brief review.* Montreal, Quebec: McGill University, 1972.

Glaser, R. (Ed.). *Training research and education.* Pittsburgh: University of Pittsburgh Press, 1962.

156 References

Glaser, R. Instructional technology and the measurement of learning outcomes: some questions. *American Psychologist* 18, 1963, 519–521.

Glaser, R. (Ed.). *Teaching machines and programed learning, II.* Washington, D.C.: National Education Association of the U.S., 1965.

Glaser, R., & Nitko, A. J. Measurement in learning and instruction. In R. L. Thorndike (Ed.), *Educational measurement.* Washington, D.C.: American Council on Education, 1971.

Guilford, J. P. *The nature of human intelligence.* New York: McGraw-Hill, 1967.

Harmes, H. M. *Behavioral analysis of learning objectives.* West Palm Beach, Florida: Harmes and Associates, 1969.

Harris, C. W. An interpretation of Livingston's reliability coefficient for criterion-referenced tests. *Journal of Educational Measurement* 9, 1972, 27–30.

Harvey, O., & Beverly, G. Some personality correlates of concept change through role playing. *Journal of Abnormal and Social Psychology* 63, 1961, 125–130.

Hausdorf, H. Empirical determination of the relative importance of educational objectives. *Journal of Experimental Education* 34, 1965, 97–99.

Haynes, J. L. Improving instruction in speech communication skills through learning hierarchies: an application to organization. *The Speech Teacher*, 22, 1973, 237–243.

Hershman, K. E. The efficacy of advance organizers and behavioral objectives for improving achievement in physics. Unpublished doctoral dissertation, Purdue University, 1971.

Hovland, C., Janis, I., & Kelley, H. *Communication and persuasion.* New Haven: Yale University Press, 1953.

Hsu, T. C. Empirical data on criterion-referenced tests. Paper presented at the meeting of the American Educational Research Association, New York, February 1971.

Jackson, R. Developing criterion-referenced tests. *T. M. Reports,* No. 15, Princeton, New Jersey: Educational Testing Service, 1970.

Janeczko, R. J. The effect of instructional objectives and general objectives on student self-evaluation and psychomotor performance in power mechanics. Unpublished doctoral dissertation, University of Missouri-Columbia, 1971.

Janis, I., & King, B. The influence of role-playing on opinion change. *Journal of Abnormal and Social Psychology* 49, 1954, 211–218.

Janis, I., & Mann, L. Effectiveness of emotional role-playing in modifying smoking habits and attitudes. *Journal of Experimental Research in Personality* 1, 1965, 84–90.

Jenkins, J. R., & Deno, S. L. Influence of knowledge and type of objectives on subject-matter learning. *Journal of Educational Psychology* 62, 1971, 67–70.

Jordan, J. S. The use of behavioral objectives in introductory college biology. Unpublished doctoral dissertation, Auburn University, 1971.

Kalish, D. M. The effects on achievement of using behavioral objectives with fifth grade students. Unpublished doctoral dissertation, Ohio State University, 1972.

Kearney, N. C. *Elementary school objectives.* New York: Russell Sage Foundation, 1953.

Kibler, R. J., & Barker, L. L. Stating objectives in speech communication. *National Association of Secondary School Principals Bulletin* 54, 1970, 30–39.

Kibler, R. J., Barker, L. L., & Cegala, D. J. Behavioral objectives and speech communication instruction. *Central States Speech Journal* 21, 1970a, 71–80.

Kibler, R. J., Barker, L. L., & Cegala, D. J. A rationale for using behavioral objectives in speech instruction. *The Speech Teacher* 19, 1970b, 245–256.

Kibler, R. J., Barker, L. L., & Miles, D. T. *Behavioral objectives and instruction.* Boston: Allyn and Bacon, Inc., 1970.

King, B., & Janis, I. Comparison of the effectiveness of improvised versus nonimprovised role-playing in producing opinion change. *Human Relations* 9, 1956, 177–186.

Krathwohl, D. R., Bloom, B. S., & Masia, B. B. *Taxonomy of educational objectives—the classification of educational goals, Handbook II: affective domain.* New York: David McKay Company, Inc., 1964.

Kriewall, T. E. Aspects and applications of criterion-referenced tests. Paper presented at the meeting of the American Educational Research Association, Chicago, April 1972.

Kueter, R. A. Instructional strategies: the effect of personality factors on recognition learning using statements of behavioral objectives as opposed to no statements of behavioral objectives prior to instruction. Unpublished doctoral dissertation, Indiana University, 1970.

Lange, P. (Ed.). *Programed instruction.* Part II. The Sixty-sixth Yearbook of the National Society for the Study of Education. Chicago: University of Chicago Press, 1967.

Lawrence, R. M. The effects of three types of organizing devices on academic achievement. Unpublished doctoral dissertation, University of Maryland, 1970.

Lazarus, A., & Knudson, R. *Selected objectives for the English language arts: grades 7–12.* Boston: Houghton Mifflin, 1967.

Lessinger, L. M. Accountability in public education. *Today's Education* 59, 1970, 52–53.

Livingston, S. A. *The reliability of criterion-referenced measures.* Report No. 73. Baltimore: Center for the Study of Social Organization of the Schools, The Johns Hopkins University, 1970.

Livingston, S. A. Criterion-referenced applications of classical test theory. *Journal of Educational Measurement* 9, 1972, 13–27.

Loh, E. L. The effect of behavioral objectives on measures of learning and forgetting on high school algebra. Unpublished doctoral dissertation, University of Maryland, 1972.

Lovett, H. T. The effects of various degrees of knowledge of instructional objectives and two levels of feedback from formative evaluation on student achievement. Unpublished doctoral dissertation, University of Georgia, 1971.

McCandless, B. R. *Children: behavior and development.* 2nd ed. New York: Holt, Rinehart and Winston, 1967.

McDonald, F. J. *Educational psychology.* 2nd ed. Belmont, California: Wadsworth, 1965.

Macdonald, J. B., & Walfron, B. J. A case against behavioral objectives. *The Elementary School Journal* 71, 1970, 119–128.

McGuire, W. J. The nature of attitudes and attitude change. In G. Lindzey and E. Aronson (Eds.), *The handbook of social psychology,* Vol. III. 2nd ed. Reading, Massachusetts: Addison-Wesley Company, 1969.

McNeil, J. D. Concomitants of using behavioral objectives in the assessment of teacher effectiveness. *Journal of Experimental Education* 36, 1967, 69–74.

Mager, R. F. *Preparing instructional objectives.* San Francisco, California: Fearon Publishers, 1962.

Mager, R. F. *Developing attitude toward learning.* San Francisco, California: Fearon Publishers, 1968.

Mager, R. F., & Beach, K. M., Jr. *Developing vocational instruction.* San Francisco, California: Fearon Publishers, 1967.

Mager, R. F., & Clark, C. Explorations in student-controlled instruction. *Psychological Reports* 13, 1963, 71–76.

Mager, R. F., & McCann, J. *Learner-controlled instruction.* Palo Alto, California: Varian and Associates, 1961.

Merrill, P. F., & Towle, N. J. The effects of the availability of objectives on performance in a computer-managed graduate course. Prepublication paper, Florida State University, 1971.

Miles, D. T., & Robinson, R. E. The general teaching model. Unpublished manuscript, Educational Research Bureau, Southern Illinois University, 1969.

Miller, R. B. Analysis and specification of behavior for training. In R. Glaser (Ed.), *Training research and education.* Pittsburgh: University of Pittsburgh Press, 1962a.

Miller, R. B. Task description and analysis. In R. M. Gagné (Ed.), *Psychological principles in system development.* New York: Holt, Rinehart and Winston, 1962b.

Morrison, H. C. *The practice of teaching in the secondary school.* Chicago: University of Chicago Press, 1926.

Nelson, D. L. The effect of specifically stated instructional objectives on the achievement of collegiate undergraduate economics students. Unpublished doctoral dissertation, University of Minnesota, 1970.

Olsen, C. R. A comparative study of the effect of behavioral objectives on class performance and retention in physical science. Unpublished doctoral dissertation, University of Maryland, 1972.

Olson, G. H. A multivariate examination of the effects of behavioral objectives, knowledge of results and assignment of grades on the facilitation of classroom learning. Unpublished doctoral dissertation, Florida State University, 1971.

Oswald, J. M., & Fletcher, J. D. Some measured effects of specificity and cognitive level of explicit instructional objectives upon test performance among eleventh grade social science students. Paper presented at the annual meeting of the American Educational Research Association, Minneapolis, 1970.

Patton, C. T. The effect of student knowledge of behavioral objectives on achievement and attitudes in educational psychology. Unpublished doctoral dissertation, University of Northern Colorado, 1972.

Phillips, J. A. The effects of instructional objectives treatment on economics achievement scores for students in selected community colleges. Unpublished doctoral dissertation, University of Southern California, 1971.

Piatt, G. R. An investigation of the effect of the training of teachers in defining, writing, and implementing educational behavioral objectives has on learner outcomes for students enrolled in a seventh grade mathematics program in the public schools. Unpublished doctoral dissertation, Lehigh University, 1969.

Popham, W. J. *Systematic instructional decision making.* Audio-tape and filmstrip, 20 minutes. Los Angeles: Vimcet Associates, 1965.

Popham, W. J. Probing the validity of arguments against behavioral goals. Paper presented at the annual meeting of the American Educational Research Association, Chicago, Illinois, February 1968.

Popham, W. J. (Ed.). *Instructional objectives: an analysis of emerging issues.* Chicago: Rand McNally, 1969.

Popham, W. J. Indices of adequacy for criterion-referenced test items. Symposium presented at the annual meeting of the American Educational Research Association and the National Council on Measurement in Education, Minneapolis, Minnesota, March 1970.

Popham, W. J., & Baker, E. L. *Establishing instructional goals.* Englewood Cliffs, New Jersey: Prentice-Hall, 1970.

Popham, W. J., & Husek, T. R. Implications of criterion-referenced measurement. *Journal of Educational Measurement* 6, 1969, 1–9.

Poulliotte, C. A., & Peters, M. G. *Behavioral objectives: a comprehensive bibliography.* Boston: Instructional Technology Information Center, 1971.

Puckett, T. J. Implementing and assessing instruction via instructional systems and behavioral objectives. Unpublished doctoral dissertation, Ohio State University, 1971.

Robinson, R. E., & Miles, D. T. Behavioral objectives: an even closer look. *Educational Technology,* 11, 1971, 39–44.

Rowan, T. E. Affective and cognitive effects of behavioral objectives. Unpublished doctoral dissertation, University of Maryland, 1971.

Scott, W. Attitude change through reward of verbal behavior. *Journal of Abnormal and Social Psychology* 55, 1957, 72–75.

Scott, W. Attitude change by response reinforcement: replication and extension. *Sociometry* 22, 1959, 328–335.

Simpson, E. J. The classification of educational objectives in the psychomotor domain. In *The psychomotor domain.* Vol. 3. Washington: Gryphon House, 1972.

Smith, J. M. Relations among behavioral objectives, time of acquisition, and retention. Unpublished doctoral dissertation, University of Maryland, 1970.

Smith, S. A. The effects of two variables on the achievement of slow learners on a unit in mathematics. Unpublished Master's thesis, University of Maryland, 1967.

Smythe, M. J., Kibler, R. J., & Hutchings, P. W. A comparison of norm-referenced and criterion-referenced measurement with implications for communication instruction. *The Speech Teacher* 22, 1973, 1–17.

Spell, G. R., Kibler, R. J., & Parks, A. M. A comparison of mastery and traditional learning systems with selected implications for speech communication instruction. Paper presented at the meeting of the International Communication Association, Atlanta, Georgia, April 1972.

Stedman, C. H. The effects of prior knowledge of behavioral objectives on cognitive learning outcomes using programmed materials in genetics. Unpublished doctoral dissertation, Indiana University, 1970.

Stolurow, L. M. *Teaching by machine.* Washington, D.C.: U. S. Government Printing Office, 1963.

Taber, J. I., Glaser, R., & Schaefer, H. H. *Learning and programmed instruction.* Reading, Massachusetts: Addison-Wesley, 1965.

Thorndike, E. L. The nature, purposes and general methods of measurements of educational products. In G. M. Whipple (Ed.), *The measurement of educational products.* Part II. Seventeenth Yearbook of the National Society for the Study of Education. Bloomington Public School Company, 1918.

Tiemann, P. W. Student use of behaviorally-stated objectives to augment conventional and programmed revisions of televised college economics lectures. Paper presented at the meeting of the American Educational Research Association, Chicago, 1968.

Tobias, S., & Duchastel, P. C. Behavioral objectives, sequence, and anxiety in CAI. Tech Memo No. 57. Tallahassee: CAI Center, Florida State University, 1972.

Tyler, R. W. *Constructing achievement tests.* Columbus: Ohio State University, 1934.

Tyler, R. W. *Basic principles of curriculum and instruction.* Chicago: The University of Chicago Press, 1950.

Tyler, R. W., Gagné, R. M., & Scriven, M. *Perspectives of curriculum evaluation.* American Educational Research Association. Monograph Series on Curriculum Evaluation. Chicago: Rand McNally, 1967.

Walbesser, H. H. *Constructing behavioral objectives.* College Park: Bureau of Educational Research, University of Maryland 1966

Wallace, J. Role reward and dissonance reduction. *Journal of Personality and Social Psychology* 3, 1966, 305–312.

Washburne, C. W. Educational measurement as a key to individual instruction and promotions. *Journal of Educational Research* 5, 1922, 195–206.

Webb, A. B. Effects of the use of behavioral objectives and criterion evaluation on classroom progress of adolescents. Unpublished doctoral dissertation, University of Tennessee, 1971.

Weinberg, H. Effects of presenting varying specificity of course objectives to students on learning motor skills and associated cognitive material. Unpublished doctoral dissertation, Temple University, 1970.

Wittrock, M. C. Set applied to student teachings. *Journal of Educational Psychology* 53, 1962, 175–180.

Wright, A. R., & Doxsey, J. R. *Measurement in support of affective education.* Salt Lake City: Interstate Educational Resource Service Center, 1972.

Zimmerman, C. L. An experimental study of the effects of learning and forgetting when students are informed of behavioral objectives before or after a unit of study. Unpublished doctoral dissertation, University of Maryland, 1972.

APPENDIX A

SAMPLES OF INSTRUCTIONAL OBJECTIVES

An efficient means of learning to write instructional objectives is to observe "models" of objectives that have been written by other teachers and curriculum planners. The purpose of this section is to provide a *variety* of such models encompassing a wide range of subject matter. All of the sample objectives included have been written for actual classroom use and, in many cases, have been published as part of a curriculum guide.

The examples include a broad range of styles and formats. Some of those objectives provided do not follow the format for writing instructional objectives that we have suggested. However, we thought that sample objectives of varying formats would be helpful to teachers in making decisions about the most desirable format to use for their purposes. The sample objectives included are not purported to be examples of "excellence" in the craft of objective formulation—they are included primarily to provide concrete examples of the types of instructional objectives that are currently in use.

PMI OBJECTIVES[1]

Given a rectangle that has been divided into a number of equal squares of which some are shaded, the student will be able to specify the fractional part of the rectangle that is shaded. (Pictorial fractions)

[1]From John Gessel, *Teacher's Guide for Use with the Prescriptive Mathematics Inventory.* Copyright © 1972 by McGraw-Hill, Inc. Reprinted by permission of the publisher, CTB/McGraw-Hill, Del Monte Research Park, Monterey, Ca., 93940. All rights reserved. Printed in U.S.A.

Given a number line showing the operation of addition of whole numbers and an appropriate open mathematical sentence, the student will be able to complete the mathematical sentence to describe the operation.

Given an addition problem with two negative integers as addends, the student will be able to supply a missing addend in the commuted form of the problem.

Given a multiplication problem with three positive fractions as factors parenthesized to show a particular grouping of factors, the student will be able to supply a missing factor in the problem parenthesized to show a different grouping of factors.

Given an equation with a missing factor, where the sum is implicit in a mixed number, the student will be able to apply the distributive property in supplying the missing factor.

Given a number less than 10 and a table of numbers such as a section of a hundreds chart, the student will be able to mark all of the multiples of the given number on the chart.

Given an illustration of an acute angle overlayed by a protractor, the student will be able to indicate the measure of the angle in degrees.

Given a drawing of a trapezoid subdivided into a parallelogram and an equilateral triangle with all dimensions shown, the student will be able to compute the area of the figure.

Given a matrix of values for an arbitrary, abstract system under an abstract operation and two equations, the second derived from the first, the student will be able to derive a third equation demonstrating the associative property for the operation. (Abstract systems)

Given a right triangle with the lengths of the sides indicated, the student will be able to specify the sine of one of the acute angles as a fraction.

EDUCATIONAL PSYCHOLOGY[2]

Upon reading the first section of this chapter (on a theory of teaching), you should be able to meet these objectives:

[2]From John P. DeCecco, *The Psychology of Learning and Instruction: Educational Psychology* © 1968. Reprinted by permission of Prentice-Hall, Inc., Englewood Cliffs, New Jersey, pp. 5 and 6, 57 and 58.

1. Indicate the three questions about teaching behavior which a theory of teaching answers and provide an illustration of a theory of teaching which raises and answers these questions.
2. Point out characteristics (in terms of questions raised and answered) which distinguish a theory of teaching from a theory of learning; describe the relationship between a theory of teaching and a theory of learning; and provide illustrations of a theory of teaching and of a theory of learning which indicate these distinctions and relationships.
3. Point out characteristics (in terms of questions raised and answered) which distinguish a theory of teaching from a philosophy of education; illustrate these distinctions by comparing a teaching theory and a philosophy of education.

Upon reading the second and third sections of this chapter (on models of teaching), you should be able to meet these objectives:

4. List the four components of the basic teaching model and illustrate how a feedback loop from performance assessment (the fourth component) results in adjustments in the three remaining components.
5. Describe the psychological teaching models of (a) Stolurow, (b) Carroll, and (c) Flanders in terms of the components of the basic teaching model.
6. Describe the historical teaching models of (a) Socrates, (b) the Jesuits, and (c) Combs and Snygg in terms of the components of the basic teaching model.

Upon reading the first section of this chapter (on the definition of entering behavior), you should be able to meet these objectives:

1. List the major characteristics of entering behavior.
2. Distinguish entering behavior from and relate it to terminal performance by pointing out similar and dissimilar characteristics.
3. Distinguish entering behavior from and relate it to readiness, maturation, individual differences, and personality by pointing out similar and dissimilar characteristics.
4. Illustrate relevant entering behavior for an instructional objective of your own choice.

VAE SYSTEMS PROJECT

VAE 5134 Advanced Typewriting[3]

Given a typewriting lesson plan, the student will evaluate it and make the following revisions:

a. develop new supplementary materials for beginning the lesson.
b. develop new consumer and job topics pertinent to the lesson.
c. if necessary, revise directions to insure clarity and precise communication.
d. if necessary, revise the presentation of content if the facts presented are not accurate.
e. if necessary, construct a closer integration between the component parts of the lesson plan.
f. if necessary, edit the plan to eliminate errors in spelling, punctuation, grammar, or syntax.
g. if necessary, make changes so that the plan conforms to the format specified for a typewriting lesson plan.

The student will demonstrate at least five of the following classroom management procedures:

a. attendance procedures.
b. distribution of materials.
c. care of equipment.
d. talking only when it is quiet.
e. chalkboard use.
f. use of instructional equipment.
g. techniques of testing (i.e., handling results, recording test scores).

Criteria for each of the above management skills will be provided. This demonstration will occur during the 40–50 minute teaching performance which takes place in actual typing classes in Metropolitan Detroit.

[3]From T. Johnson, R. Richey, and B. Moy, *VAE Pre-Certification Teacher Education Program: Competencies & Performance Objectives,* Series No. 1. Detroit: Wayne State University, 1972, pp. 728–39. Reprinted by permission of the authors.

The student will teach one 40–50 minute typing lesson to secondary students in the Metropolitan Detroit area. The groups may be either small groups or total typing classes. The lesson for this teaching experience will be:

a. written according to the VAE format incorporating the specified components of a typing lesson plan.
b. either revised lessons dealt with in class or newly developed plans.
c. based upon entry level job skills.
d. incorporated into the sequence of lessons currently being taught by the existing teacher in that classroom.
e. approved by the VAE instructor and the classroom teacher.
f. utilize demonstration and questioning techniques as well as other appropriate delivery systems if possible.

The teaching performance will be evaluated on the following basic teaching skills:

a. beginning a lesson.
b. clarity of presentation.
c. pupil participation and attention.
d. questioning skills.
e. pacing of the lesson.
f. selection and use of supplementary materials, including:
 (1) the use of transparencies according to the specifications provided
 (2) thought starters
 (3) quality of the reproduction of handouts
 (4) ASA drills.
g. ending lesson.

In addition, this teaching performance task will be evaluated using scores from 3–5 minute exit tests or products which measure the lesson's performance objectives. Finally, a statement will be provided from the classroom teacher that the pre-intern has passed the objective.

The student will identify new ideas on how to teach typewriting from at least five articles written within the last five years which deal with classroom experiments or practical experiences. Each article must be summarized using the Turabian annotation format. The five articles must each deal with a differenct topic from the following areas of instruction:

a. upper alphabetic keys.
b. lower alphabetic keys
c. home row keys.
d. numeric and special keys.
e. margins.
f. horizontal centering.
g. vertical centering.
h. tabulations.
i. letters and memos.
j. erasing.
k. crowding and spreading.
l. composing at the typewriter.

VAE 5187 Methods and Materials of Instruction I[4]

Using the projected teaching specialization as a basis for content selection and the unit plan format developed in objective #07146, the student will develop a written unit teaching plan which includes a preface describing the specific teaching situation for which the unit plan has been designed. Topic #6 in *Teaching Successfully* along with student selected references should be used as a guide for the development of the unit teaching plan. A project teaching plan may be developed as a unit teaching plan.

Using the example of safety instruction for the engine lathe on pages 408–411 of *Teaching Successfully*, the student will prepare in written outline form the safety instruction for a machine that would be included in the laboratory equipment of the projected teaching specialization.

Using Topic #3 of *Teaching Successfully* and current reference materials, the students will analyze possible learner handicaps that they will probably need to deal with in an industrial education laboratory. These would include consideration for learners who are left-handed or with

a. defective vision.
b. impaired hearing.
c. a speech defect.

[4]From G. Harold Silvius and Arthur Deane, *VAE Pre-Certification Teacher Education Program: Competencies and Performance Objectives*, Series No. 1. Detroit: Wayne State University, 1972, pp. 728–57. Reprinted by permission of the authors.

d. a crippled condition.
e. poor mental health.

Using the projected teaching specialization and Topics #9 & #10 of *Teaching Successfully* as a guide, the student will develop written criteria for evaluating text, reference, and visual materials (transparencies, films, etc.) for a specific learning situation. The criteria will be written in standard outline format. The outline of criteria will include a preface briefly describing the learning situation for which the criteria have been developed. The students' ability to analyze a given situation involving student handicaps will be evaluated on the course examination.

Using the projected teaching specialization and the text, *Teaching Successfully,* as a guide, the student will design a *total record keeping system* which could be adapted to future classroom/laboratory experiences. This record keeping system should include

a. class books.
b. individual progress charts.
c. accident reports.
d. safety records.
e. informal pertinent data concerning students.
f. other pertinent records which the student feels are needed to administer the projected teaching specialization.

The format for the record keeping system will follow the form of a standard written outline. The outline will include a preface that describes the learning situation for which the record keeping system has been designed.

SELF CONCEPT OBJECTIVES: Primary Level[5]

Direct Self Report

Objective No. 1. (Comprehensive) Students will evidence positive self concepts by indicating agreement with questions that reflect positive

[5]From Instructional Objectives Exchange, *Measures of Self Concept: K–12.* Rev. ed. Los Angeles: Instructional Objectives Exchange, 1972, pp. 19–21, 26–28. Reprinted by permission of the Instructional Objectives Exchange.

perceptions of the self in relation to family, peers, scholastic achievement, and about the self in general; and by indicating disagreement with questions that reflect negative perceptions of self in these areas.

Objective No. 2. (Peer) Students will display positive self concepts in the peer dimension by indicating agreement with questions that reflect positive peer relations or positive perceptions of the self in social situations; and by indicating disagreement with negative questions.

Objective No. 3. (School) Students will evidence positive self concepts in the school dimension by expressing agreement with questions concerned with success or perceived esteem in scholastic endeavors; and by indicating disagreement with questions concerned with perceived failure or lack of achievement.

Objective No. 4. (Family) Students will exhibit positive self concepts in the family dimension by indicating agreement with questions that present positive perceptions of self in terms of family relationships or situations; and by indicating disagreement with negative questions.

Objective No. 5. (General) Students will evidence positive self concepts about the self in general by expressing agreement with questions that depict a person with positive self esteem; and by indicating disagreement with questions that depict a person with negative self esteem.

Inferential Self Report

Objective No. 6. (General) Students will display positive self concepts by indicating their *willingness* to play a wide variety of roles in an imaginary television show, when given the opportunity to select an unlimited number of parts which they would play.

Objective No. 7. (Peer) Students will display positive self concepts by indicating that others would choose them to play roles which carry positive images in a pretend play.

Objective No. 8. (Family) Students will display positive self concept by selecting responses that indicate that their mothers would not dislike them if they engaged in actions usually expected to yield parental disapproval.

Observational Indicators

Objective No. 9. When given the opportunity to display classwork, students will give evidence of positive self concepts by voluntarily posting their work.

Objective No. 10. Given a contrived situation in which the teacher describes a group of fictitiously esteemed students, class members will demonstrate positive self concepts by voluntarily identifying themselves as students who belong to this group.

OBJECTIVES FOR ATTITUDES RELATED TO TOLERANCE: GRADES 9–12[6]

Objective 1: Students will indicate agreement with statements indicative of a tolerant attitude toward others, and disagreement with statements indicative of an intolerant attitude toward others. Tolerance is here considered to be the willingness not to interfere with the activities of others and the rejection of cultural stereotypes.

Objective 2: Students will indicate agreement with statements indicative of a desire to seek out unfamiliar social and cultural situations, and disagreement with statements indicative of a rejection of such experiences.

Objective 3: Students will indicate acceptance of a variety of policy statements which have been judged to express tolerance of the values and opinions of others, and opposition to statements judged to reflect intolerant policies.

Objective 4: Students will indicate disagreement with statements tending to stereotype beliefs and behavior of people within cultural groups, and agreement with statements suggesting that individuals vary significantly within such groups.

Objective 5: Given hypothetical situations concerning a generalized other and alternative reactions the student will select the reactions indicative of a desire or willingness to associate with people of different racial groups, to see people of different racial groups in favorable status situations, and to see them as dominant or successful. In cases of illegal or detrimental behavior the student will select reactions indicative of a rejection of such behavior.

Objective 6: Given hypothetical situations and alternative reactions the student will select the reactions indicative of tolerance toward certain

[6]From Instructional Objectives Exchange, *Attitudes Related to Tolerance: Grades 9–12.* Los Angeles: Instructional Objectives Exchange, 1971, pp. 13–16. Reprinted by permission of the Instructional Objectives Exchange.

behavior and personal beliefs of people of given races. Tolerance as measured here is defined as the willingness not to interfere in the beliefs or activities of others.

Objective 7: Given a list of positive and negative statements about specific races the student will reflect positive attitudes by selecting the alternative "very many" in response to how many of the people possess each positive characteristic and "very few" in response to how many possess each negative characteristic.

Objective 8: Students will, when given a series of hypothetical situations and alternative solutions, select the solutions which have been judged to reflect a tolerant attitude toward the values and opinions of others.

Objective 9: Given a series of hypothetical situations concerning specific races or other people in general and alternative reactions, the student will select the responses which reflect a tolerant attitude.

SAMPLE INSTRUCTIONAL OBJECTIVES FOR THE LANGUAGE ARTS[7]

Given a set of kernel sentences with an adjective in the predicate, the student will identify the predicate and the adjective.

Given a group of incomplete sentences requiring adjectives, the student will supply adjectives to complete the sentences.

Given incomplete sentences which include a choice of pronouns in different cases, the student will select the pronoun in the correct form to complete the sentence.

Given a set of compound sentences, the student will (1) identify the independent clauses in each sentence and (2) identify the conjunction which connects them.

Given orally a list of spelling words containing three-letter blends, the students will (1) spell the words correctly; (2) underline the blend; and (3) organize the words by rewriting them into appropriate grouping under one of the following labels: *str, thr, squ, spl, scr, spr.*

Given kernel sentences with a blank space in the subject and/or object position, the student will select and write the correct personal pronoun to complete each sentence.

Given a list of singular nouns and a set of rules for forming noun plurals, the student will select the appropriate rule for forming the noun plural

[7]From Instructional Objectives Exchange, *Language Arts 4–6.* Los Angeles: Center for the Study of Evaluation, UCLA Graduate School of Education, 1966. Reprinted by permission of the Instructional Objectives Exchange.

for each of the singular nouns, write the correct plural for that noun, and write the numerical representation of the rule for plural formation which governs each noun.

Given a list of base nouns, the student will: (1) in one column add the morpheme *ful* to each base noun; (2) in a second column write each word thus created with stress marks to demonstrate the pronunciation; and (3) in a third column indicate whether each newly formed word is a noun or an adjective according to its stress pattern. The *adjective* has the stress pattern, "first-weak"; the *noun* has the stress pattern, "first-second."

Given the rules for capitalization and a set of twelve sentences which contain no capitalization, the student will rewrite each sentence using the appropriate capitalization, and identify the rule for each change by writing the rule after the sentence.

Given a set of rules for the use of the colon and a set of sentences which require insertion of colons, the student will place each colon properly and identify the rule appropriate to each placement.

Given an oral conversation through dictation, the student will record the conversation in written form, observing and using established paragraph form, and supplying in the appropriate places quotation marks, capital letters, and terminal punctuation.

Given an assignment to write a three-paragraph theme about three separate but related objects, the student will demonstrate his understanding of proper paragraphing by writing about each of the objects in a separate paragraph. The paragraphs will conform to prespecified criteria. Paragraph form is defined as an indented first line and paragraph unity is defined as all sentences pertaining to the topic idea.

The student will write a fictional story about a particular country based upon factual information taken from the encyclopedia. The story should have a main character, and should include action or details which are both consistent with the country described and representative of that country.

Given an assignment to develop a story plot, the student will write a story incorporating the following criteria:

1. He will include at least two characters, with the main character involved in a challenge or a struggle.
2. He will include a climax to the story which results from the presentation of details in a sequential order.
3. He will include a climax which is determined by and prepared for by the events of the story.

APPENDIX B

PROGRAM TEXT DESIGNED TO TEACH STUDENTS HOW TO USE INSTRUCTIONAL OBJECTIVES

Our experiences in using instructional objectives suggest that students learn more efficiently and effectively when they first are taught how to use instructional objectives. The programed text contained in this section is intended to be general in terms of the subject matter and evaluation procedures used with objectives, but specific to the instructional objective format presented in chapter 2. The teacher may be required to modify the program to suit his/her particular style of objective writing, content, and/or evaluation procedures. The program is designed to serve as an example. We encourage you either to use the program in its current form or to develop one for your particular needs.

INTRODUCTION

The following program is designed to teach you how to use instructional objectives. If this program is successful, after completing it, you should be able to:

1. State the five components of instructional objectives;

2. Identify the five components of instructional objectives given to you by your teacher;
3. Use instructional objectives to prepare for tests and study more effectively.

1

Instructional objectives are statements that describe what students will be able to do after completing a prescribed unit of instruction. For example, an instructional objective for a unit in history might be: "Given 30 minutes, the student will be able to list in writing three major factors which gave rise to the Industrial Revolution."

Instructional objectives are important to you as a student because they inform you:

1. What information is important to learn.
2. How you will be asked to demonstrate that you have learned the required material.

—Go to the Next Frame—

2

Instructional objectives are_____
_____.
They are important to students because _____.

1.

2.

—Go to the Next Frame—

3

Your responses to the preceding frame should have been: *Instructional objectives are statements that describe what students will be able to do after completing a prescribed unit of instruction.* They are important to you as students because *they inform you:*

1. *What information is important to learn.*
2. *How you will be asked to demonstrate that you have learned the required material.*

—Go to the Next Frame —

4

While the particular format of instructional objectives may vary from teacher to teacher, all good instructional objectives have in common components informing students what is to be learned and how learning is to be demonstrated.

In this program we will examine five components of instructional objectives:

1. *Who* is to perform the desired behavior (e.g., "the student").
2. The *actual behavior* to be employed in demonstrating mastery of the objective (e.g., "to write," "to speak").
3. The *result* (i.e., the product or performance) of the behavior, which will be evaluated to determine whether the objective is mastered (e.g., "an essay" or "the term paper").
4. The *relevant conditions* under which the behavior is to be performed (e.g., "in a one-hour quiz" or "in front of the class").
5. The *standard* that will be used to evaluate the success of the product or performance (e.g., "90 percent correct" or "four out of five correct").

—Go to the Next Frame—

5

The five components of instructional objectives are:

1. _____
2. _____
3. _____
4. _____
5. _____

—Go to the Next Frame—

6

Your response to Frame 5 should look something like this:

1. Who is to perform the desired behavior (e.g., "the student").
2. The actual behavior to be employed in demonstrating mastery of the objective (e.g., "to write," "to speak").
3. The result (i.e., the product or performance) of the behavior, which will be evaluated to determine whether the objective is mastered (e.g., "an essay" or "the term paper").
4. The relevant conditions under which the behavior is to be performed (e.g., "in a one-hour quiz" or "in front of the class").
5. The standard that will be used to evaluate the success of the product or performance (e.g., "90 percent correct" or "four out of five correct").

—Go the Next Frame—

7

Here are the five components of instructional objectives:

1. Who is to perform the desired behavior.
2. The actual behavior to be employed in demonstrating mastery of the objectives.
3. The result (i.e., product or performance) of the behavior, which will be evaluated to determine whether the objective is mastered.
4. The relevant conditions under which the behavior is to be performed.
5. The standard that will be used to evaluate the success of the product or performance.

Examine the following objective, and see if you can identify the five components of instructional objectives (underline each component and place the number—i.e., 1–5—of the component above that which corresponds to the portion of the objective you have underlined).

Given a list of 20 pairs of chemical compounds and/or elements, the student will provide in writing complete chemical reactions for 80 percent of the pairs using the standard sym-

bols as indicated in the textbook.

—Go the Next Frame—

8

Your response should look like this:

4
Given a list of 20 pairs of chemical compounds and/or ele-
1   2   3
ments, the student will provide in writing complete chemical
5
reactions for 80 percent of the pairs using the standard sym-

bols as indicated in the textbook.

1. Who is to perform the desired behavior.
2. The actual behavior to be employed in demonstrating mastery of the objectives.
3. The result (i.e., product or performance) of the behavior, which will be evaluated to determine whether the objective is mastered.
4. The relevant conditions under which the behavior is to be performed.
5. The standard that will be used to evaluate the success of the product or performance.

Well, how did you do? If you were unable to identify all of the five components, don't worry.

—Go to the Next Frame—

9

There should be little or no problem in identifying the first component of instructional objectives (i.e., who is to perform the behavior), since it will always be YOU—the student. However, you probably will encounter a variety of actual behaviors, results, relevant conditions, and standards in objectives that teachers present to you. To help you use instructional objectives most efficiently, let us examine each of these components more closely to see exactly what information you should obtain from each component.

—Go to the Next Frame—

10

As you know, the second component of instructional objectives informs students of the *actual behavior* to be employed in demonstrating mastery of the objective. Examples of typical "action verbs" used by teachers to communicate this message to students are listed below:

1. identifying	6. describing
2. distinguishing	7. stating a rule
3. constructing	8. applying a role
4. naming	9. demonstrating
5. ordering	10. interpreting

—Go to the Next Frame—

11

It is important that you become sensitive to the type of information provided for you by the second component (i.e., actual behavior) of instructional objectives. Consider the following objectives. Rank the objectives from 1–3 on the relative difficulty of the behavior required to demonstrate mastery of each objective [using 1 as being the most difficult].

1. Given 20 math problems, the student will apply the distributive law in solving at least 18 problems correctly.
2. Given 20 minutes, the student will list in the correct order the steps a bill must go through before becoming a law.
3. Given 20 minutes, the student will write an essay comparing and contrasting at least three types of government.

—Go to the Next Frame—

12

We would rank the objectives as follows. How do your rankings compare? If they are the same as below, go to frame 14, if not, go to the next frame (13).

1. Given 20 minutes, the student will write an essay comparing and contrasting at least three types of government.
2. Given 20 math problems, the student will apply the distributive law in solving at least 18 problems correctly.
3. Given 20 minutes, the student will list in the correct order the steps a bill must go through before becoming a law.

13

Look at the three objectives again:

1. Given 20 minutes, the student will write an essay comparing and contrasting at least three types of government.
2. Given 20 math problems, the student will apply the distributive law in solving at least 18 problems correctly.
3. Given 20 minutes, the student will list in the correct order the steps a bill must go through before becoming a law.

Note that the first objective indicates that you will be expected "to write an essay comparing and contrasting. . . ." In our estimation, this would appear more difficult than merely listing steps in the correct order or applying the same rule to several problems. Writing an essay would involve organizing and expressing thoughts clearly in addition to demonstrating knowledge about the topic of the essay.

Similarly, applying a rule in solving math problems would appear more difficult than merely listing steps in the correct order. One could simply memorize the steps in correct order, but one cannot memorize how to apply a math rule to unique problems.

One method for utilizing the information provided by the second component of instructional objectives is to ask yourself: (1) exactly what is it that you are required to *do,* and (2) how would you study most efficiently to enable you to perform the required behavior.

—Go to the Next Frame—

14

The third component of instructional objectives indicates the product or performance that will be evaluated by the teacher. This component is particularly important because it often conveys specific information about what is to be studied. For example, consider the objectives below; underline the part of each objective that conveys information about the product or performance that is to be evaluated:

1. Given 20 minutes, the student will correctly translate at least 20 out of 25 Spanish words into their English equivalents.
2. Given 10 minutes, the student will draw a model of communication and label each component in the model.
3. Given a bar graph of production rate, the student will write an essay comparing and contrasting the rate of production over a 5-year period.

–Go to the Next Frame–

15

Your responses should look something like this:

1. Given 20 minutes, the student will correctly translate at least 20 out of 25 Spanish words into their English equivalents.
2. Given 10 minutes, the student will draw a model of communication and label each component in the model.
3. Given a bar graph of production rate, the student will write an essay comparing and contrasting the rate of production over a 5-year period.

If your responses match with ours, go to Frame 17; if not, go to Frame 16.

16

Examine the objectives again:

1. Given 20 minutes, the student will correctly translate at least 20 out of 25 Spanish words into their English equivalents.
2. Given 10 minutes, the student will draw a model of communication and label each component in the model.
3. Given a bar graph of production rate, the student will write an essay comparing and contrasting the rate of production over a 5-year period.

Note that in the first objective the result of the student behavior (i.e., translating) is a list of *Spanish words with their English equivalents.* The result of the student behavior always is the product or performance—that is, the third component of instructional objectives.

Similarly, the result of drawing in the second objective is *a model of communication* with *each component* labeled. In the third objective the result of comparing and contrasting is *an essay on the rate of production over a five-year period.*

Got it?!!

—Go to the Next Frame—

17

The fourth component of instructional objectives indicates the conditions under which the required behavior is to be performed: for example, how much time you will be given; whether you will be given any reference materials, etc. It is sometimes difficult for a teacher to include all of the conditions under which a given behavior will be performed. However, good objectives contain at least the most essential information regarding the conditions under which the behavior is to be demonstrated. For example:

1. When presented with a typed list . . .
2. Given a slide rule and 20 minutes . . .
3. Without any reference materials or notes . . .
4. Given a tape recording . . .
5. Given a reference book . . .

—Go to the Next Frame—

18

Individuals sometimes confuse the fourth and fifth components of instructional objectives. We already know that the fourth component conveys information about the relevant conditions under which the behavior will be demonstrated. But what was that fifth component?

—Go to the Next Frame—

19

The fifth component of instructional objectives is *the standard (or criterion) that will be used to evaluate your performance.*

Certainly this is an important bit of information for a student to know. The standard indicates what a correct response is and how correct a response must be before it is considered acceptable. Examine the following objective, and underline the part indicating the standard of evaluation.

Given one hour and no reference materials, the student will

write an essay synthesizing the causes and consequences of

World War II. The essay must contain at least three of the

major causes and three of the major consequences that were

discussed in the textbook.

—Go to the Next Frame—

20

Your response should look like this:

Given one hour and no reference materials, the student will

write an essay synthesizing the causes and consequences of

World War II. <u>The essay must contain at least three of the</u>

<u>major causes and three of the major consequences that were</u>

<u>discussed in the textbook.</u>

How did you do? Try to identify the standard in these objectives:

1. Given a list of 20 unpunctuated sentences, the student will rewrite each sentence and correctly punctuate at least 18 of the 20 sentences.
2. Given 100 words presented orally, the student will spell correctly at least 85 percent of the words.
3. Given a 100-word business letter, the student will type the letter within 1½ minutes and make no errors.

—Go to the Next Frame—

21

Your response should look like this:

1. Given a list of 20 unpunctuated sentences, the student will rewrite each sentence and correctly punctuate <u>at least 18 of the 20 sentences.</u>
2. Given 100 words presented orally, the student will spell correctly <u>at least 85 percent</u> of the words.
3. Given a 100-word business letter, the student will type the letter <u>within 1½ minutes and make no errors.</u>

—Go to the Next Frame—

22

At this point you should be reasonably familiar with the five components of instructional objectives and what kind of information each component provides you.

You should keep in mind that teachers often have different ways of stating objectives, so you may not always find all of the components we have discussed. However, all good instructional objectives will inform you: (1) what information is important to learn and (2) how you will be asked to demonstrate that you have learned the required material.

—Go to the Next Frame—

23

In summary, describe what information is conveyed by the following objective:

Given a diagram of an internal combustion engine and one hour, the student will label at least 80 percent of the components of the diagram and describe how they function.

_____

_____

_____

_____

—Go to the Next Frame—

24

While the wording may differ, your response should indicate the following points:

1. That you will be provided with a diagram of an internal combustion engine.
2. That you will be given an hour to produce the required product.
3. That the product consists of a diagram with labeled components and a description of how each component functions.
4. That at least 80 percent of the components in the diagram must be labeled and described before the answer is acceptable.

THE END

APPENDIX C

INSTRUMENTATION OF BLOOM'S AND KRATHWOHL'S TAXONOMIES FOR THE WRITING OF EDUCATIONAL OBJECTIVES[1]

During the past six or eight years an increased amount of attention has been given to the statement of educational objectives in behavioral terms both to facilitate the evaluation of educational programs and to improve the validity of the measures and scales utilized in the evaluation process (Metfessel and Michael, 1967; Michael and Metfessel, 1966). Although set up as a programmed learning text, Mager's (1962) *Preparing Instructional Objectives* has been one of the most useful guides to teachers and specialists in curriculum who have sought help in stating the desired outcomes of instruction in behavioral language—in describing the kinds of specific and relatively terminal behaviors which the learner will be capable of exhibiting subsequent to his exposure to a program of instruction. Another useful source has been the volume edited by Lindvall (1964) who, in collaboration with Nardozza and Felton (Lindvall, Nardozza, and Felton, 1964) not only prepared his own chapter concerned with the importance of specific objectives in curricular development, but also enlisted the aid of several

[1]Newton S. Metfessel, W. B. Michael, and D. A. Kirsner, "Instrumentation of Bloom's and Krathwohl's Taxonomies for the Writing of Educational Objectives," *Psychology in the Schools* 6, 1969, 227–231. This article is reprinted by permission, for which the authors express their thanks.

distinguished educators, e.g., Krathwohl (1964) and Tyler (1964) with specialized interests in evaluation. Such efforts have essentially involved a fusion of curriculum design with the evaluation process in that curricular planning is described in terms of behavioral objectives that are necessary for the construction of valid tests and scales. The taxonomies provide the required model necessary to furnish meaningful evidence regarding the attainment of desired behavioral changes.

Although Krathwohl (1964) related the taxonomy of educational objectives in both the cognitive (Bloom, 1956) and the affective (Krathwohl, Bloom, and Masia, 1964) domains to curriculum building, he was able to present only a limited number of concrete illustrations, some of which Mager would probably challenge because of their relative lack of specificity. Admittedly, Krathwohl has made an important and helpful start in relating objectives to a meaningful and rather well-known conceptual framework. However, the writers believe that there exists a need for an instrumentation of the taxonomy of educational objectives within both the cognitive and affective domains—that is, a more clear-cut description of how the taxonomy can be implemented in the school setting. The approach utilized was the development of *behaviorally oriented* infinitives which, when combined with given objects, would form a basis for meaningful, cohesive, and operational statements.

PURPOSE

Thus the essential purpose of this paper was to show how specific behavioral objectives can be formulated within the hierarchy of the major levels and sublevels of the taxonomies of educational objectives as set forth by Bloom (1956) and Krathwohl (1964). Such a framework should furnish a helpful base around which behavioral statements of objectives can be formulated.

Definition

An educational objective consists of a description of the behaviors of an individual (the learner or examinee) in relation to his processing information embodied in subject matter—that is, what the learner must be capable of doing with certain characteristics or properties of subject matter. The behavioral component, which may be described as a process involved at an appropriate level of the taxonomic classification, is usually expressed in the form of a noun "ability" or a verb of being "able" followed by an infinitive such as the "ability to do" or "able to do." The second component of the objective, which consists of the specific content often found in the formal learning experience (e.g., in the curricular or instructional unit), constitutes a direct object of the verb or infinitive form. The terms "subject matter" or "content" are used in a fairly broad sense, as their level of specificity is highly variable, depending upon the characteristics of the curricular unit.

INSTRUMENTATION

To facilitate the formulation of statements of specific behavioral objectives within the framework of Bloom's taxonomy, the writers have included a table made up of three columns. The first column contains the taxonomic classification identified by both code number and terminology employed in Bloom's (1956) taxonomy. The entries in the second column consist of appropriate infinitives which the teacher or curriculum worker may consult to achieve a precise or preferred wording of the behavior or activity desired. In the third column somewhat general terms relative to subject matter properties are stated. These direct objects, which may be expanded upon to furnish specificity at a desired level, may be permuted with one or more of the infinitive forms to yield the basic structure of an educational objective—activity (process) followed by content (subject matter property). At the discretion of the reader the words "ability" or "able" can be inserted in front of each of the infinitives.

Although within a given major process level or sublevel of the taxonomy each infinitive cannot in all instances be meaningfully or idiomatically paired with every direct object listed, many useful permutations of infinitives and direct objects that furnish entirely readable statements are possible. Certainly use of these tables should lead to a substantial gain in the clarity and speed with which teachers and curriculum specialists, as well as those involved in construction of achievement tests, may state curricular objectives. The writers have found that these tables have been of considerable help to their students, as well as to personnel in public

TABLE I INSTRUMENTATION OF THE TAXONOMY OF
EDUCATIONAL OBJECTIVES:
COGNITIVE DOMAIN

Taxonomy Classification	KEY WORDS Examples of Infinitives	Examples of Direct Objects
1.00 Knowledge		
1.10 Knowledge of Specifics		
1.11 Knowledge of Terminology	to define, to distinguish, to acquire, to identify, to recall, to recognize	vocabulary, terms, terminology, meaning(s), definitions, referents, elements
1.12 Knowledge of Specific Facts	to recall, to recognize, to acquire, to identify	facts, factual information, (sources), (names), (dates), (events), (persons), (places), (time periods), properties, examples, phenomena
1.20 Knowledge of Ways and Means of Dealing with Specifics		
1.21 Knowledge of Conventions	to recall, to identify, to recognize, to acquire	form(s), conventions, uses, usage, rules, ways, devices, symbols, representations, style(s), format(s)
1.22 Knowledge of Trends, Sequences	to recall, to recognize, to acquire, to identify	action(s), processes, movement(s), continuity, development(s), trend(s), sequence(s), causes, relationship(s), forces, influences
1.23 Knowledge of Classifications and Categories	to recall, to recognize, to acquire, to identify	area(s), type(s), feature(s), class(es), set(s), division(s), arrangement(s), classification(s), category/ categories

TABLE I (Continued)

KEY WORDS

Taxonomy Classification	Examples of Infinitives	Examples of Direct Objects
1.24 Knowledge of Criteria	to recall, to recognize, to acquire, to identify	criteria, basics, elements
1.25 Knowledge of Methodology	to recall, to recognize, to acquire, to identify	methods, techniques, approaches, uses, procedures, treatments
1.30 Knowledge of the Universals and Abstractions in a Field		
1.31 Knowledge of Principles, Generalizations	to recall, to recognize, to acquire, to identify	principle(s), generalization(s), proposition(s), fundamentals, laws, principal elements, implication(s)
1.32 Knowledge of Theories and Structures	to recall, to recognize, to acquire, to identify	theories, bases, interrelations, structure(s), organization(s), formulation(s)
2.00 Comprehension		
2.10 Translation	to translate, to transform, to give in own words, to illustrate, to prepare, to read, to represent, to change, to rephrase, to restate	meaning(s), sample(s), definitions, abstractions, representations, words, phrases
2.20 Interpretation	to interpret, to reorder, to rearrange, to differentiate, to distinguish, to make, to draw, to explain, to demonstrate	relevancies, relationships, essentials, aspects, new view(s), qualifications, conclusions, methods, theories, abstractions
2.30 Extrapolation	to estimate, to infer, to conclude, to predict, to differentiate, to determine, to extend, to interpolate, to extrapolate, to fill in, to draw	consequences, implications, conclusions, factors, ramifications, meanings, corollaries, effects, probabilities

TABLE I (Continued)

| | KEY WORDS | |
Taxonomy Classification	Examples of Infinitives	Examples of Direct Objects
3.00 Application	to apply, to generalize, to relate, to choose, to develop, to organize, to use, to employ, to transfer, to restructure, to classify	principles, laws, conclusions, effects, methods, theories, abstractions, situations, generalizations, processes, phenomena, procedures
4.00 Analysis		
4.10 Analysis of Elements	to distinguish, to detect, to identify, to classify, to discriminate, to recognize, to categorize, to deduce	elements, hypothesis/ hypotheses, conclusions, assumptions, statements (of fact), statements (of intent), arguments, particulars
4.20 Analysis of Relationships	to analyze, to contrast, to compare, to distinguish, to deduce	relationships, interrelations, relevance, relevancies, themes, evidence, fallacies, arguments, cause-effect(s), consistency/consistencies, parts, ideas, assumptions
4.30 Analysis of Organizational Principles	to analyze, to distinguish, to detect, to deduce	form(s), pattern(s), purpose(s), point(s) of view(s), techniques, bias(es), structure(s), theme(s), arrangement(s), organization(s)
5.00 Synthesis		
5.10 Production of a Unique Communication	to write, to tell, to relate, to produce, to constitute, to transmit, to originate, to modify, to document	structure(s), pattern(s), product(s), performance(s), design(s), work(s), communications, effort(s), specifics, composition(s)

TABLE I (Continued)

	KEY WORDS	
Taxonomy Classification	Examples of Infinitives	Examples of Direct Objects
5.20 Production of a Plan, or Proposed Set of Operations	to propose, to plan, to produce, to design, to modify, to specify	plan(s), objectives, specification(s), schematic(s), operations, way(s), solution(s), means
5.30 Derivation of a Set of Abstract Relations	to produce, to derive, to develop, to combine, to organize, to synthesize, to classify, to deduce, to develop, to formulate, to modify	phenomena, taxonomies, concept(s), scheme(s), theories, relationships, abstractions, generalizations, hypothesis/hypotheses, perceptions, ways, discoveries
6.00 Evaluation		
6.10 Judgments in Terms of Internal Evidence	to judge, to argue, to validate, to assess, to decide	accuracy/accuracies, consistency/consistencies, fallacies, reliability, flaws, errors, precision, exactness
6.20 Judgments in Terms of External Criteria	to judge, to argue, to consider, to compare, to contrast, to standardize, to appraise	ends, means, efficiency, economy/economies, utility, alternatives, courses of action, standards, theories, generalizations

schools who are concerned with writing objectives prior to curriculum development, constructing test items, or to carrying out evaluation studies. Slight modifications can be made with the entries to meet the requirements of specific learning situations.

INSTRUMENTATION: AFFECTIVE DOMAIN

The instrumentation of the Affective Domain is the same as that of the Cognitive Domain, to wit, the selection of behaviorally oriented infinitives

combined with selected direct objects. As in the case of the Cognitive
Domain, these are to be conceptualized as examples for the stimulation of
other infinitives and objects and, more important, meaningful objectives in
a total framework.

TABLE II INSTRUMENTATION OF THE TAXONOMY OF EDUCATIONAL OBJECTIVES: AFFECTIVE DOMAIN

Taxonomy Classification	KEY WORDS Examples of Infinitives	Examples of Direct Objects
1.0 Receiving		
1.1 Awareness	to differentiate, to separate, to set apart, to share	sights, sounds, events, designs, arrangements
1.2 Willingness to Receive	to accumulate, to select, to combine, to accept	models, examples, shapes, sizes, meters, cadences
1.3 Controlled or Selected Attention	to select, to posturally respond to, to listen (for), to control	alternatives, answers, rhythms, nuances
2.0 Responding		
2.1 Acquiescence in Responding	to comply (with), to follow, to commend, to approve	directions, instructions, laws, policies, demonstrations
2.2 Willingness to Respond	to volunteer, to discuss, to practice, to play	instruments, games, dramatic works, charades, burlesques
2.3 Satisfaction in Response	to applaud, to acclaim, to spend leisure time in, to augment	speeches, plays, presentations, writings
3.0 Valuing		
3.1 Acceptance of a Value	to increase measured proficiency in, to increase numbers of, to relinquish, to specify	group membership(s), artistic production(s), musical productions, personal friendships

TABLE II (Continued)

	KEY WORDS	
Taxonomy Classification	Examples of Infinitives	Examples of Direct Objects
3.2 Preference for a Value	to assist, to subsidize, to help, to support	artists, projects, viewpoints, arguments
3.3 Commitment	to deny, to protest, to debate, to argue	deceptions, irrelevancies, abdications, irrationalities
4.0 Organization		
4.1 Conceptualization of a Value	to discuss, to theorize (on), to abstract, to compare	parameters, codes, standards, goals
4.2 Organization of A Value System	to balance, to organize, to define, to formulate	systems, approaches, criteria, limits
5.0 Characterization by Value or Value Complex		
5.1 Generalized Set	to revise, to change, to complete, to require	plans, behavior, methods, effort(s)
5.2 Characterization	to be rated high by peers in, to be rated high by superiors in, to be rated high by subordinates in	humanitarianism, ethics, integrity, maturity
	and	
	to avoid, to manage, to resolve, to resist	extravagance(s), excesses, conflicts, exorbitancy/ exorbitancies

APPENDIX D

SOURCES FOR INSTRUCTIONAL OBJECTIVES: NATIONAL CLEARINGHOUSES

While we encourage teachers at all levels of education (i.e., elementary, secondary, and higher) to prepare and use instructional objectives, we recognize that teachers often are too burdened by the demands of their day-to-day job of education to embark on the difficult, time-consuming task of personally constructing instructional objectives and related evaluation measures. Fortunately, other educators have recognized this potential problem and have organized national clearinghouses that make available instructional objectives and corresponding evaluation measures to teachers in several different subject areas. Following is a list of these national clearinghouses to which interested teachers may write and obtain information about the availability of instructional materials relevant to their particular subject areas. We strongly encourage all teachers concerned with instruction to support these clearinghouses by *contributing* their instructional objectives and evaluation measures and by *withdrawing* objectives and test items that are suitable for their particular instructional situation

OBJECTIVES   SOURCE

All subject areas Instructional Objectives Exchange
                   P.O. Box 24095
                   Los Angeles, California 90024

OBJECTIVES   SOURCE

All subject areas *UNIPAC Objectives*
                   Institute for the Development of Educational
                       Advancement
                   (IDEA) University of California
                   Suite 950
                   1100 Glendon Avenue
                   Los Angeles, California 90024

All subject areas *Fort Lincoln New Town Objectives (FLINT)*
                   General Learning Corporation
                   5454 Wisconsin Avenue, NW
                   Washington, D. C. 20015

Special purpose   *Nova Objectives*
   objectives   Mr. Warren Smith
                   Nova High School
                   36 Southwest 70th Avenue
                   Fort Lauderdale, Florida 33313

Math, Science,   *IPI Objectives*
   Reading   Dr. Robert Scanlon
                   1700 Market Street
                   Philadelphia, Pennsylvania 19103

Math   *PRIMES Objectives*
                   Doris Cresswell
                   Educational Research Associates
                   Bureau of General and Academic Education
                   Department of Education
                   Box 911
                   Harrisburg, Pennsylvania 17126

Math   *Clark County Objectives*
                   Clark County School District
                   2832 East Flamingo Road
                   Las Vegas, Nevada 89109

Math   *Individualized Mathematics System Objectives (IMS)*
                   Mr. Edwar Bruchak
                   Regional Education Lab for the Carolinas &
                       Virginia
                   613 Vickers
                   Durham, North Carolina 27701

OBJECTIVES   SOURCE

Math, Science,   *LRA Objectives*
  & Specific   Learning Research Associates
  Reading (not   1501 Broadway
  yet available)   New York, New York 10036

All subject areas   *Directory of Sources of Measurement Objectives*
  Dr. John Ahlenius
  Consultant
  Assessment and Evaluation
  State Office Building
  Denver, Colorado 80203

INDEX